75⁰

BAR & GRILL
COOKBOOK

BAR & GRILL COOKBOOK

*Exciting New Recipes from
San Francisco's
Bar & Grill Restaurants*

James McNair

■

Photography by Tom Tracy

CHRONICLE BOOKS • SAN FRANCISCO

For my sister Martha,
with thanks for plunging right into this project as soon
as you moved to California. It's a long way from Jones-
ville, Louisiana catfish, but I hope you and John will feel
at home in this state of glorious beauty, unparalleled
bounty, and creative freedom that has made California
host to America's most innovative ideas, including the
great cooking celebrated in this volume.

Printed in Japan

Library of Congress
Cataloging-in-Publication Data

San Francisco bar & grill.

  Includes index.
  1. Barbecue cookery. 2. Hotels, taverns,
etc.—California—San Francisco.
I. McNair, James K.
II. Title: San Francisco bar & grill.
TX840.B3S26 1986   641.7'6 86-8293
ISBN 0-87701-370-5

Editorial and photography production
by The Rockpile Press, Lake Tahoe and
San Francisco

Photography designed by James McNair
Styling by Martha McNair
Editorial production assistance by Lin Cotton
Photography assistance by Bob Brandon
and Chris Saul
Copy editing by Carolyn Miller

Book and cover design by
Thomas Ingalls + Associates
Typography by On Line Typography

Chronicle Books
One Hallidie Plaza
San Francisco, California 94102

CONTENTS

THE BAR & GRILL

"*T*HE COUNTRY'S newest culinary excitement is coming out of San Francisco's gourmet grills," stated James Villas in *Town and Country* magazine about the time I began this book. Perhaps "newest" is the wrong word since this uniquely San Francisco type of restaurant is nearly as old as the fabled City itself.

Good food and drink have been synonymous with the City of San Francisco since mining, logging, and the railroad created a world-class city practically overnight. In spite of all the current fanfare over "California cuisine," grilling, and ethnic foods, these essential elements of the San Francisco dining experience actually go about as far back as the City itself. Grills with open fire pits are documented among the first restaurants in the tent and shack San Francisco of 1849. Fresh meat, game, or fish was purchased by the customer on the premises or from adjoining marketplaces and cooked to order.

The pursuit of gold brought cooks from around the world to the developing San Francisco. Almost from the beginning there were establishments offering the foods of China, Italy, France, England, Spain, Germany, Holland, Chile, Peru, Mexico, and other corners of the globe. Each added their own cooking techniques and introduced new food products and seasonings to the 1850s bar & grills of San Francisco. Through the years the City remained a cosmopolitan center, evidenced by its choice as the birthplace of both the League of Nations and the United Nations. Today, dishes of the entire world are prepared as authentically as possible or modified to feature local products. Ethnic ingredients and techniques are a major part of the late-1980s bar & grills. You can enjoy grilled fish fresh from nearby waters and sauced with a choice of Italian-style *pesto,* French-style *beurre blanc,* Thai-style peanut sauce, or New Mexican roasted-chili salsa.

Today San Francisco bar & grills fall into two categories: the traditional landmark grills along with a few imitators, and the new breed of trendy upscale cafe-grills. Both types are favorite haunts of locals and food-loving visitors alike.

Perry's.

Rings.

Fog City Diner.

Campton Place.

A few of the early restaurants that dubbed themselves grills still thrive: Tadich (1849), Jack's (1864), and Sam's (1867). These original "San Francisco experience" restaurants have always featured immaculately fresh fish and shellfish, cooked and served with simplicity. While these landmarks still maintain their popularity by devotion to quality ingredients and old-time atmosphere, highly innovative variations on the theme are meeting success throughout the City and America.

Bustling young San Francisco quickly faced a shortage of good cooks. San Francisco historian Doris Muscatine notes that anyone with even modest kitchen talent could make more money than a reasonably lucky miner. Millionaire François Pioche brought over forty Paris-trained chefs to help meet the demand of the youthful city hooked on dining out. Today, San Francisco has no shortage of cooking talent. The bold styles of well-educated and experimental young chefs have updated an old tradition and created the new-style cafe-grills, birthplaces of "California cuisine." The dining-out experience has become a new form of theater in San Francisco, with chefs assuming the role of stars.

In this volume, media-focused and award-winning chefs and restaurateurs Joyce Goldstein (Square One), Bradley Ogden (Campton Place), Cindy Pawlcyn (Fog City Diner), and Patricia Unterman (Hayes Street Grill) are joined by Bobby Estenzo (Prego), James Geof Felsenthal (Rosalie's), Julie Ring (Rings), and others destined for stardom in the glamorous new world of food.

Authentic California cuisine, dating from the beginnings of San Francisco, has always placed emphasis on the finest and freshest local ingredients, enhanced with an enormous variety of food products grown or imported for California's multi-ethnic communities. For all the press fanfare, "new California cuisine" follows a long tradition of San Francisco cooking, updated by creative chefs devoted to quality and working with newly available produce and other ingredients. Due to the influence of nouvelle cuisine, attention is given to presentation as well as flavor.

Backyard grilling has long been immensely popular in California, where the mild climate allows outdoor cooking almost year round. It was only natural that the distinct flavors of aromatic wood fuels be brought indoors by California restaurants. Mesquite cookery, which has spread as far from the City as Manhattan and most points in between, is identified by many as the characteristic component of San Francisco grills. Mesquite wood or charcoal comes from a scrubby tree in arid regions of North and South America, where it's been the primary cooking fuel of peasants for centuries. Mesquite is prized for its delicate aroma and ability to start out hotter and maintain an even heat longer than conventional charcoal. Although recently made chic, mesquite has been supplied by Lazzari Fuel Company to San Francisco grills for over thirty years. In spite of the City's reputation as the mesquite cookery capital, many San Francisco grills opt for gas or a combination of gas and varied wood fuels.

In addition to mesquite-grilled meats, fowl, fish, and vegetables, hallmarks of the newer upscale cafe-grills include pasta, *polenta,* pizza and *calzone,* domestic caviars, fresh wild mushrooms and truffles, roasted red peppers, chilies, abundant garlic, fresh salsas, crisply cooked baby vegetables, exotic fruits, uncommon garden greens (or "designer lettuces," as dubbed by some), warm salads, and the world of fresh herbs, especially pungent cilantro. When dining in cafe-grills, San Franciscans have learned to expect the unexpected in ingredient combinations, cooking methods, and presentation; surely no other city has found as many things to do with goat's milk cheese.

I choose to define "bar & grill" as a San Francisco original, a distinct style of American restaurant with roots in the French bistro and the Italian *trattoria,* where fresh, simply prepared foods are featured in a homey atmosphere, often where conviviality reigns. As you'll note from the pages that follow, the bar & grill can't be stereotyped. It can run the gamut from neon-lighted, raucous yuppie palaces to quiet, semiprivate, wood-panelled traditional dining rooms. In common, they all feature the use of a grill. Service is nonformal and a bit relaxed, usually by a young, friendly staff, with the bistro apron replacing the tuxedo.

Hayes Street Grill.

The first recorded use I've found of the term "bar & grill" in San Francisco came in 1973 when Ed and Mary Etta Moose opened Washington Square Bar & Grill, affectionately coined "the Washbag" by *San Francisco Chronicle* columnist Herb Caen. More than a decade later, when this popular watering hole was severely attacked by a local restaurant reviewer, Caen accurately defined many "barngrills" when he wrote defensively that the critic "seemed not to understand that the regulars go there for something besides the food. Friendship, warmth, noise, fairly decent shouted conversation, a great staff. A place to go when one is alone in the lonely city."

Ciao.

While excellent bar-cafe-grills now fill the surrounding communities of the Bay Area, the state of California, and as far away as New York City, I have chosen to limit this book to establishments within the confines of San Francisco itself, the place where it all began. However, homage must be paid to Berkeley, and especially to Alice Waters' Chez Panisse, where an old tradition was rekindled with a fresh spirit and the "new" style of grill cookery was popularized. Here was the training ground for many of the new breed of chefs who've found their way to the City. Quite a few personalities in this book are Chez Panisse alumni.

Prego.

I've selected a variety of San Francisco establishments to illustrate the bar & grill experience. Some are personal favorites that I can recommend wholeheartedly; others are crowd pleasers that reflect dining trends and offer good food although they may be too noisy, smoky, or pricy for my taste. Hopefully, all will still be in business long after publication of this book; however, the nature of the restaurant business is such that today's hot spot may be tomorrow's faded memory.

Many establishments that call themselves bar & grills do not fit my image of the genre and have not been included here. Fake flowers, unattended plants, or shabby decor demonstrates a lack of attention to freshness and detail. Absent are the few places where the prima donna temperament of the chef or staff overshadows the dining experience. Rudeness, incompetent service, too-limited selections, overpricing for value given, and of course, poor quality of food do not make it in my book.

Almost everyone who's looked over my list of bar & grills has questioned the absence of Stars, one of San Francisco's most popular spots. Alas, Jeremiah Tower's publisher would not allow him to give out any more recipes. His own book offers a taste of the type of dishes he created at Balboa Cafe, Santa Fe Bar & Grill, and Stars.

Some restaurants that are included do not use the words *bar* or *grill* in their name, but are true examples of traditional or innovative grill cookery. Perhaps unexpectedly, two hotel dining rooms—the understated and too-often-overlooked Cafe Bedford and the luxuriously elegant Campton Place—have been included because they represent American grill cooking at its finest.

You'll find some departures from the commonplace uses of the grill: Harris', an idea transplanted to Van Ness Avenue from the famed Harris Ranch, serves grilled prime beef in a sophisticated Old San Francisco clubhouse atmosphere; Gaylord, overlooking the Bay in Ghiradelli Square, is a comfortable and picturesque spot for the ancient *tandoori* grilling of India, and its bar features comfortable sofas and coffee tables; Ciao and Prego, both originated by Jerry Magnin's Spectrum Foods empire, grill Italian style and feature rarely imported Italian wines, while L'Entrecote de Paris grills in the style of France and offers favorite French vintages. I'd hoped to include a Japanese, Korean, or other Asian-style grill, but have not discovered one that meets all my qualifications.

I've chosen Sam's Grill, which has cooked over mesquite for decades before it became the trendy fuel, to represent the surviving handful of traditional fish grills. Genial owner-host Gary Seput recognized Sam's role in inspiring the grill concept and is amused at the idea of much-touted open kitchens being something new; Sam's kitchen has long been on display. The Hayes Street Grill is a fine example of an updated variation on this theme.

Fresh and exciting Rings in the revitalized South of Market area, glitzy Rosalie's with its Hollywood-set decor, and the cozy Zuni Cafe with its Southwestern motif are examples of the "new" California cuisine. Cooking at these three has heavily ethnic overtones and an emphasis on the changing seasons.

Architecturally sleek Square One features hearty international classics, while the chromed and neoned Fog City Diner updates an American institution.

MacArthur Park, Perry's, and Washington Square Bar & Grill emphasize the convivial bar, yet offer good grill fare.

In each case, the chefs and/or owners have supplied menus, beverage suggestions, and recipes for meals that serve from four to a dozen. Their selections of food and drink capture the distinct flavor and character of their establishments.

In a city notorious for the drinking habits of the citizenry, a word about the "bar" portion of the bar & grill is important. In compiling this book, it has become quite obvious that the drinking habits of San Franciscans have changed. Wines, including aperitifs and champagnes, have all but replaced the old standby cocktails as before-dinner drinks. When cocktails are chosen, San Franciscans prefer their booze straight, on the rocks, or with simple mixers. Fitness-conscious people are choosing bubbly mineral water, plain or splashed with wine, before meals. Both mineral water and wine continue to flow throughout the meal. Reflecting these trends, several of the restaurants in this volume do not have bars in the traditional sense, but feature excellent wine lists. In addition to the standard house wines, many bar & grills now offer a selection of premium wines by the glass, allowing patrons to experiment inexpensively with matching foods and wines.

White wines, mostly from California, still lead the popularity poll, but several bartenders report the increasing popularity of reds. While chef-owner Joyce Goldstein of Square One feels her hearty foods are best paired with red wine, customers still order more white. Only Zuni's bartender reported red wines as more popular than white.

Spicy grilled food often calls for icy cold beer, accounting for the growing appreciation for this drink among patrons of San Francisco's bar & grills.

When you choose to entertain in the bar & grill manner, the word to remember is simplicity. The photographs in this book are filled with atmospheric suggestions that can be adapted to home dining. Interesting tabletops of wood, stone, or metal can be left uncovered. Otherwise, plain linens in white or the currently popular pink are appropriate. For authenticity, avoid patterned fabrics; an exception is the classic blue and white check seen at Perry's.

Zuni Cafe.

As you'll note in the food closeups, bar & grill planners favor plain white dishes, but you might choose other neutral colors such as the beige of Wedgwood Drabware, or terra-cotta, celadon, or black, which shows off food dramatically. Patterned china should be avoided if you're after the casual bar & grill look.

If used at all, tabletop decorations in the bar & grill are kept minimal. One or a few seasonal blossoms in bottles or narrow-mouthed vases does it. Many purist restaurateurs keep tabletops plain to show off the food, opting for large-scale flower bouquets elsewhere in the dining area. For this effect at home, display masses of flowers or bold splashes of exotic blossoms in urns or pots on sideboards, pedestals, or mantels.

It is my wish that you use this collection of menus and restaurant-tested recipes, all adapted to the home kitchen, to capture the essence of bar & grill dining San Francisco style. You'll discover a variety of styles, all dedicated to good food and good times.

Rosalie's.

CAFÉ BEDFORD

*L*IKE SO MANY other food pros today, Stephen Tumbas, creator of the Café Bedford, is highly educated in other fields, holding degrees in both Russian and French. Time spent in France converted him to the enjoyment and study of good food, so he returned to San Francisco to study hotel management at City College. After a stint as the St. Francis Hotel banquet manager, he moved to the country to manage the Harris Ranch restaurant, but after three years yearned again for city life and that American dream of owning his own restaurant. The opportunity came when real estate investor Bill Kimpton, the mastermind behind the renovation of several small old hotels in San Francisco, offered Tumbas the Bedford Hotel dining room. Café Bedford opened for breakfast in 1982, adding dinner about a year later.

Tumbas believes strictly in working only with the best available produce, meats, and fish, and actually grows some of the cafe's vegetables and many herbs at home. "Treat ingredients with respect," is his advice. "Simple cooking lets the natural flavors come through. Essentially our food is good basic food with balanced compositions of flavors, colors, and textures. Service should also be unpretentious."

Like the food and service, the setting is simple. Huge ficus trees tower into the two-story ceiling to soften a space that's large enough to allow plenty of elbow room. Black draperies tied back with fat gray tassled ropes, and flower drawings silk screened on acrylic sheets are set off against pale-gray walls. Café Bedford is a place for unhurried dining and quiet conversation against a background of classical music.

Chef James Murko, a graduate of the Culinary Institute of America, Hyde Park, New York, gradually worked his way across the country to San Francisco, where he cooked in private clubs before meeting Steven Tumbas. He's provided a choice of menus here for home entertaining: one appropriate for spring or early summer, and the other more suited to cold weather.

Chef James Murcko's Menus for Six

AUTUMN MENU

Baked Oysters with Corn Bread Stuffing

Fleur de Guebwiller Gewürztraminer, Schlumberger, 1983

□

Roasted Pheasant with Wild Rice Flan and Madeira Sauce

Saintsbury Pinot Noir, Carneras, 1983

□

Apple Bread Pudding with Maple Sauce

OPPOSITE: A spacious, refurbished hotel dining room is home to Cafe Bedford. ABOVE: Morels crown roasted pheasant accompanied by a custard of wild rice nested in braised red cabbage.

BAKED OYSTERS WITH CORN BREAD STUFFING

½ pound bacon (about 6 thick slices), chopped
½ cup diced celery
½ cup diced leek
½ cup diced onion
½ cup sliced fresh mushrooms
1 garlic clove, chopped
⅓ cup chopped fresh parsley
1¼ cups yellow cornmeal
¾ cup all-purpose flour
2 teaspoons double-acting baking powder
1 tablespoon sugar
½ teaspoon salt
1 egg, lightly beaten

1 cup buttermilk
½ cup (1 stick) butter, melted
1 cup cooked corn kernels
24 oysters, in shells
Rock salt
Curly endive leaves
Lemon wedges (garnish)

Cook bacon until all fat is rendered. Reserve bacon and strain grease into a sauté pan or skillet; add celery, leek, onion, mushrooms, garlic, and parsley and sauté until tender. Reserve.

Preheat oven to 400° F.

Mix cornmeal, flour, baking powder, sugar, and salt in a mixing bowl. Combine egg, buttermilk, ¼ cup melted butter, and sautéed vegetables in a separate bowl, then quickly stir into dry ingredients with as few strokes as possible. Fold in corn and reserved bacon, pour into a buttered 8-inch-square pan, and bake in oven until golden but still moist inside, about 20 minutes. Cool, then crumble slightly.

Reduce oven heat to 350° F.

Shuck oysters, reserving bottom half of shell. Place oysters-on-the-half-shell on a baking sheet spread with rock salt. Spoon 3 tablespoons corn bread mixture on each oyster. Heat in oven until warmed through.

Baked oysters covered with corn bread stuffing.

To serve, spoon remaining ¼ cup melted butter evenly over oysters and arrange on a platter with curly endive and lemon wedges. Pass as appetizers with pre-dinner drinks, or serve on individual plates as a first course.

Serves 6.

ROASTED PHEASANT WITH WILD RICE FLAN AND MADEIRA SAUCE

3 pheasants
1¼ cups vegetable oil
⅓ cup each finely chopped celery, carrot, and onion
½ cup Madeira
2 quarts water
Salt
Freshly ground black pepper
1½ cups California wild rice
1 bay leaf
1 onion, diced
4 ounces fresh mushrooms, sliced (preferably shiitakes, chanterelles, morels, or other wild types)
1 tablespoon butter
3 tablespoons chopped fresh parsley
¼ cup freshly grated Parmesan
3 cups heavy cream
Zest of 1 orange, minced
5 egg yolks
3 whole eggs

Remove wings, neck, and giblets from pheasants. Reserving livers, chop wings, neck, and giblets roughly and brown in ¼ cup oil in a 2-quart pot over medium-high heat with chopped celery, carrot, and onion. Deglaze pan with Madeira, scraping bottom. Add 1 quart water, bring to boil, reduce heat to low, and simmer slowly, skimming frequently, until reduced by half. Strain stock into a bowl, discarding pheasant parts and vegetables. Put stock in a blender or food processor, turn on, add reserved pheasant livers, and purée until sauce is thick and creamy. Strain and season to taste with salt and pepper. Reserve.

Preheat oven to 325° F.

Heat remaining 1 cup oil in large sauté pan or skillet over medium-high until smoking. Salt and pepper pheasants to taste; sear and brown in oil, turning for even color. Transfer to an ovenproof pan and roast until internal temperature reaches 135° F.

Cook rice with bay leaf in remaining 1 quart water until *al dente;* strain to remove any extra water. In a sauté pan or skillet over medium heat, cook onion and mushrooms in butter until tender, about 5 minutes. Add to rice along with parsley and Parmesan.

Increase oven to 350° F.

To make custard, combine cream with orange zest in a saucepan and warm over low heat. Lightly beat yolks and whole eggs in a bowl, add warm cream, and season to taste with salt and pepper.

Equally distribute rice mixture among 6 buttered and floured individual soufflé dishes, loosely filling each dish three-fourths of the way. Finish filling each dish with custard mixture. Place in a shallow baking pan and add 1 inch of boiling water. Cover with aluminum foil and bake until a tester comes out clean, about 45 minutes.

Cut legs and thighs from pheasants. Bone thighs and slice thinly. Cut breasts off birds and thinly slice diagonally. To serve, unmold rice flans and place one in center of each plate. Position leg and fan sliced pheasant around rice. Spoon reserved sauce over pheasant. Serve with red cabbage braised with juniper berries.

Serves 6.

Chef James Murcko (left) and owner Stephen Tumbas.

APPLE BREAD PUDDING WITH MAPLE SAUCE

¾ cup (1½ sticks) butter
6 apples, peeled, cored, halved, and thinly sliced
½ cup brandy
¼ cup currants
3 tablespoons ground cinnamon
½ teaspoon ground nutmeg
½ teaspoon ground ginger
½ teaspoon ground cloves
½ teaspoon ground allspice
4 whole eggs
6 egg yolks
2½ cups heavy cream
1½ cups plus ⅓ cup sugar
1 tablespoon vanilla extract
1 cup all-purpose flour
½ cup chopped walnuts
1 1-pound baguette, crust trimmed, sliced ¼ inch thick
Maple Sauce (recipe follows)

Heat ¼ cup butter in a sauté pan or skillet over medium-high heat. Add apple slices, brandy, currants, 1 tablespoon cinnamon, nutmeg, ginger, cloves, and allspice and cook until apples are *al dente,* about 10 minutes. Reserve.

To make custard, lightly beat whole eggs and yolks in a mixing bowl. Add cream, 1½ cups sugar, and vanilla. Stir until thoroughly mixed; reserve.

Using hands, make a streusel topping by mixing flour and walnuts with remaining ½ cup butter, ⅓ cup sugar, and 2 tablespoons cinnamon in a bowl. Reserve.

Preheat oven to 350° F.

Butter an 8-inch casserole or 8 individual custard dishes, sprinkle with sugar, and layer with half of bread. Add half of apple mixture, remainder of bread, then rest of apple mixture. Pour custard over all and top with streusel mixture. Place casserole or custard dishes in a large pan and add boiling water to halfway up container sides. Bake until a tester comes out clean, about 1¼ hours for a large casserole; about 45 minutes for individual dishes. Spoon out pudding from casserole; serve individual portions in baking dishes or invert onto plates. Serve warm with Maple Sauce.

Serves 6 to 8.

MAPLE SAUCE

1½ cups pure Vermont maple syrup
¼ cup brandy
1 cup heavy cream, warmed

Combine maple syrup and brandy in a saucepan over medium-high heat and cook until reduced by half or until syrup starts to darken, about 7 to 8 minutes. Add heated cream and stir until smooth. Serve warm.

Makes about 1¾ cups.

SPRING MENU

Sautéed Crab Cakes
with Mustard Dressing
Martin Brothers Sauvignon Blanc,
Paso Robles, 1983

□

Grilled Swordfish
with Mexican Grapefruit Salad
William Wheeler Chardonnay,
Sonoma, 1984

□

Lemon Custard Tart
with Seasonal Fruits

SAUTÉED CRAB CAKES WITH MUSTARD DRESSING

2 eggs, lightly beaten
½ cup heavy cream
About 3 cups bread crumbs, processed from thin
  French-style baguette
½ cup each julienne-cut red, green, and golden sweet
  peppers
½ cup chopped red onion
1 garlic clove, chopped
2 tablespoons butter
¼ cup dry white wine
1 pound fresh crab meat, picked over
¼ cup chopped fresh parsley
2 tablespoons chopped fresh tarragon
3 tablespoons Dijon-style mustard
Freshly squeezed lemon juice
Salt
Freshly ground black pepper
1 egg mixed with ⅓ cup milk
About ½ cup vegetable oil (for sautéing)
Mustard Dressing (recipe follows)
Watercress (garnish)

Lightly mix beaten eggs, cream, and 1 cup bread crumbs in a bowl; reserve.

In a sauté pan or skillet over medium-high heat, combine peppers, onion, and garlic with butter and white wine and cook until vegetables are tender, about 10 minutes. Combine with reserved crumb mixture. Add crab, parsley, tarragon, mustard, and lemon juice, salt, and pepper to taste. Mix well and chill for 1 hour.

Preheat oven to 400° F.

Form chilled crab mixture into 12 oval patties, dip into egg-milk mixture, and then into remaining bread crumbs. Sauté in hot oil in an oven-proof skillet until golden, turning once, about 2 minutes per side. Transfer pan to preheated oven to finish cooking, about 5 minutes. Drain crab cakes well on paper towels.

To serve, place 2 crab cakes each on individual plates with dressing alongside and garnish with watercress.

Serves 6.

MUSTARD DRESSING

1 tablespoon ketchup
½ cup plain yogurt
½ cup Dijon-style mustard
¼ cup sour cream
1 teaspoon prepared horseradish
2 tablespoons sweet pickle relish
1 tablespoon chopped fresh chives
1 hard-cooked egg, chopped
½ teaspoon cayenne pepper

Combine all ingredients in a bowl and refrigerate until serving time.

Makes about 1¾ cups.

GRILLED SWORDFISH WITH MEXICAN GRAPEFRUIT SALAD

1 tablespoon chopped fresh cilantro
2 green onions, chopped
2 fresh serrano chilies, chopped
2 tablespoons freshly squeezed lime juice
6 tablespoons olive oil
6 6-ounce swordfish steaks
1½ teaspoons coriander seeds
1½ teaspoons whole cumin seeds
3 Ruby Red grapefruits, peeled and segmented
¾ cup julienne-cut jícama
3 green onions, cut diagonally into 1-inch pieces
¾ cup julienne-cut tomatillos, fresh or canned
½ red sweet pepper, cut into julienne
½ bunch fresh cilantro, whole leaves picked from stems
1 large ripe tomato, cut into small dice
1 teaspoon honey
Salt
Freshly ground black pepper
1 avocado, sliced, or a favorite recipe for guacamole (garnish)
Sour cream (garnish)
12 corn tortillas, cut into wedges and fried in vegetable oil until crisp

In a shallow non-reactive bowl, combine chopped cilantro, chopped green onions, 1 chopped chili, lime juice, and olive oil. Add swordfish and marinate in the refrigerator for 1 hour, turning several times. Return fish to room temperature before grilling.

Toast coriander and cumin seeds in a small skillet over medium-high heat, stirring constantly until golden, about 5 minutes. Pour onto a plate to cool, then grind in a mortar. Reserve.

In a mixing bowl, combine grapefruit, jícama, sliced green onions, tomatillos, sweet pepper, remaining chopped chili, cilantro leaves, ground coriander and cumin seeds, tomato, honey, and salt and pepper to taste. Toss gently to avoid breaking grapefruit segments. Marinate 1 hour before serving.

Prepare coals or preheat broiler.

Frequently basting with its marinade, grill swordfish over high charcoal flames or under a preheated broiler, turning once until fish flakes with a fork and center is barely opaque, about 5 minutes on each side. To serve, spoon grapefruit salad over one half of each swordfish steak. Garnish with avocado slices or a scoop of guacamole, sour cream, and fried tortillas.

Serves 6.

LEMON CUSTARD TART WITH SEASONAL FRUIT

3 whole eggs
5 egg yolks
Grated zest and juice of 3 lemons
1¼ cups sugar
1 tablespoon dry vermouth
1 tablespoon unsalted butter
1 cooked 10-inch tart shell (use your favorite recipe)
About 2 cups mixed fresh seasonal fruits (whole or sliced berries, sliced papayas, mangos, kiwis)

Combine whole eggs, yolks, lemon zest and juice, sugar, and vermouth in a stainless steel bowl set over a pot of simmering water and cook, stirring constantly, until custard is thick and coats a metal spoon, about 20 minutes. Add butter and stir until melted. Strain into cooked tart shell and top with fruit. Chill until custard is set. Serve cool or at room temperature.

Serves 6.

Seasonal fruits decorate lemon custard-filled tart.

CAMPTON PLACE

*C*AMPTON PLACE is a stylish combination of contemporary and traditional decor. The appointments are lavish, the china Wedgwood, the accessories Oriental, the atmosphere elegant, the prices high, the noise level a welcome low. Although it is closely akin to a formal dining room, I've included Campton Place as a bar & grill because of the cooking style and philosophy of the chef.

Campton Place, actually the dining room of the Campton Place Hotel just off Union Square, is the showcase of Bradley Ogden, one of America's most celebrated chefs, who arrived in San Francisco amid much press fanfare. An honors graduate of the Culinary Institute of America, Hyde Park, New York, Ogden leaped into the national spotlight while cooking at the acclaimed American Restaurant in Kansas City. Ever since, he's been a leading exponent of the new spirit of American cooking that updates and glorifies our regional products and traditions.

Unfortunately, diners don't always find the chef in residence at Campton Place. He's frequently demonstrating his skills at numerous food symposiums and on television shows including a stint as guest chef on Julia Child's "Dinner at Julia's." When he's not cooking on the line, however, rest assured that he's left his kitchen well trained to maintain his high standards.

The mesquite grill is an integral part of Bradley Ogden's cooking, as evidenced in the salad of grilled shrimp and scallops and the entrée of grilled wild turkey breast offered here.

Bill Wilkinson, President of Ayala Hotels, created the small, luxurious Campton Place Hotel as "an oasis of peace and calm in the midst of bustling Union Square." Both the restaurant, open for breakfast, lunch, and dinner, and the elegant bar, a cozy setting for a rendezvous, add to the serenity.

Chef Bradley Ogden's Menu for Six

Grilled Shrimp and Scallop Salad
with Wild Rice and Cranberry Relish

☐

Grilled Wild Turkey Breast with Smoked Bacon
and Mustard Thyme Butter

Glazed Apples

Butternut Squash Gratin

Robert Mondavi Reserve Fumé Blanc, 1981
or Eyire Pinot Noir, 1983

☐

Orange Custard
with Warm Compote of Berries

OPPOSITE: *Chef Bradley Ogden.* ABOVE: *Grilled wild turkey breast with smoked bacon served with glazed apples and a gratin of butternut squash. Corn bread sticks and scones (recipes not included) accompany.*

Elegantly appointed Campton Place dining room.

GRILLED SHRIMP AND SCALLOP SALAD WITH WILD RICE AND CRANBERRY RELISH

¾ cup plus 2 tablespoons olive oil
¼ cup plus 1 tablespoon freshly squeezed lemon juice
2 tablespoons plus 2 teaspoons freshly cracked black pepper
2½ teaspoons kosher salt
18 medium-sized shrimp, peeled and deveined, tails left on
2½ cups (approximately 1 pound) bay scallops, tough strip of white muscle pulled off and discarded
¾ cup wild rice
¼ cup brown rice
¼ cup finely diced carrot
¼ cup finely diced onion
¼ cup finely diced celery
1 tablespoon plus 2 teaspoons minced garlic
2 bay leaves
1 tablespoon minced fresh thyme, or ½ teaspoon dried thyme
3 cups homemade chicken stock or canned low-sodium broth

½ cup diced green onions, white part only
¼ cup finely diced red onion
¼ cup finely diced green sweet pepper
¼ cup finely diced red sweet pepper
¼ cup chopped fresh parsley
½ teaspoon dry mustard
¼ cup thinly sliced shallots
⅓ cup red wine vinegar
1 head radicchio, leaves separated (garnish)
Cranberry Relish (recipe follows)
6 sprigs fresh thyme (garnish)

Prepare coals or preheat broiler.

Combine ¼ cup olive oil, ¼ cup lemon juice, 1 tablespoon cracked pepper, and 1 teaspoon salt in a small bowl. Add shrimp and scallops, turning to coat. Skewer and grill over glowing coals or under a preheated broiler until scallops are opaque and shrimp are pink and opaque, about 4 to 5 minutes. Reserve.

Preheat oven to 350° F.

Heat 2 tablespoons olive oil in a heavy-bottomed ovenproof pan over medium-high heat, add wild and brown rice, and sauté to coat rice with oil, about 2 minutes. Add carrot, onion, and celery and sauté lightly, about 2 minutes more. Add 1 tablespoon garlic, bay leaves, thyme, 2 teaspoons cracked pepper, 1 teaspoon salt, and chicken stock. Bring to a boil and cover. Transfer pan to oven until all liquid has been absorbed, about 45 minutes. Remove bay leaves and let cool.

After rice mixture has completely cooled, add green and red onions, green and red peppers, and parsley. Toss lightly and reserve.

To make dressing, combine mustard, shallots, remaining 2 teaspoons garlic, ½ teaspoon salt, 1 tablespoon pepper, ½ cup olive oil, vinegar, and 1 tablespoon lemon juice. Add to salad, tossing lightly to coat. Reserve.

To serve, place 2 leaves of *radicchio* on one half of each of 6 dinner plates and arrange some scallops and 3 shrimp on leaves. On other half of plates, place reserved wild rice mixture. Garnish with Cranberry Relish and a sprig of fresh thyme.

Serves 6.

CRANBERRY RELISH

1/4 cup sugar
1/2 cup port wine
Grated zest and juice of 2 lemons
Grated zest and juice of 1 orange
1/8 teaspoon ground cloves
1/8 teaspoon ground ginger
Pinch of ground nutmeg
1 1/2 cups fresh cranberries

Combine sugar, port, lemon and orange zest and juices, cloves, ginger, and nutmeg in a small saucepan over high heat. Bring to a boil, then reduce to medium heat and simmer for 5 minutes. Add cranberries and cook just until they start to burst, about 2 minutes. Remove from heat and cool.

Makes about 1 1/2 cups.

GRILLED WILD TURKEY BREAST WITH SMOKED BACON

1 cup dry white wine
1 1/2 cups apple cider vinegar
2 cups applejack brandy
1/4 cup sugar
2 teaspoons coarsely ground black pepper
2 tablespoons mustard seeds
2 tablespoons coarsely chopped garlic
1/2 cup peanut oil
6 fresh sage sprigs
8 fresh rosemary sprigs
12 fresh thyme sprigs
1 teaspoon kosher salt
1 1/2 pounds wild turkey breast, fresh or frozen (see note)
Peanut oil
Salt
Coarsely ground black pepper
6 smoked bacon slices, cut into 2-inch pieces
Mustard Thyme Butter (recipe follows)

Coffee service at the bar.

To prepare marinade, combine white wine, vinegar, 1½ cups brandy, sugar, black pepper, and mustard seeds in a saucepan. Place over high heat and bring to a boil. Continue boiling until mixture is reduced by half. Remove pan from heat and set aside to cool. Add garlic, oil, sage, rosemary, thyme, and salt.

Place turkey breast in a casserole dish and pour marinade over meat. Cover tightly and refrigerate for 2 days, turning meat twice a day.

After marinating, remove turkey breast from casserole. Strain marinade, add remaining ½ cup brandy, and reserve for basting.

Prepare coals or preheat broiler.

Pat turkey dry, then lightly rub with peanut oil, salt, and pepper to taste. Place on a grill over low coals or under a slow preheated broiler. Without allowing grease to flare up, sear breast on one side, then roll it to the other side, making sure that both sides are crisp and golden brown. Continue to grill, basting with marinade, until meat reaches an internal temperature of 160° F, about 25 to 30 minutes. Remove from heat and let meat rest for about 10 minutes before carving.

Sauté bacon until it is crisp but retains some juices. Reserve.

Preheat 6 dinner plates.

To serve, slice turkey breast into 18 slices. Place 3 pieces on each preheated plate with 1 teaspoon of Mustard Thyme Butter and 3 pieces of crisped bacon. Serve with Glazed Apples and Butternut Squash Gratin.

Serves 6.

NOTE: Wild turkey will average 6 to 8 pounds per bird. The meat is quite lean, and darker than a domestic turkey with a somewhat gamier flavor. If using frozen turkey, thaw it overnight in refrigerator. Remove breast and tie it with butcher twine to retain its shape while marinating.

Etched glass establishes the swan logo motif.

MUSTARD THYME BUTTER

1 tablespoon fresh thyme leaves, chopped
6 tablespoons unsalted butter, softened to
    room temperature
3 tablespoons Dijon-style mustard
1/2 teaspoon kosher salt
1/4 teaspoon ground black pepper
Juice of 1/2 lemon

Combine all ingredients, mixing well. Cover
and refrigerate until serving time.

Makes about 1/2 cup.

BUTTERNUT SQUASH GRATIN

3 tablespoons unsalted butter
1/2 medium-sized yellow Spanish onion, quartered and
    sliced 3/8 inch thick
Salt
Freshly ground black pepper
1 teaspoon minced or pressed garlic
3 cups 1/4- to 3/8-inch-thick peeled butternut squash
    slices (about 2 pounds whole squash)
1 1/2 cups heavy cream
1/2 cup half and half
2 bay leaves
3 fresh thyme sprigs, or 1/8 teaspoon ground dried thyme
1/8 teaspoon ground mace
2 teaspoons kosher salt
1/2 teaspoon freshly ground black pepper
1/4 cup freshly grated Parmesan cheese

Place a heavy-bottomed sauté pan or skillet over
medium heat and add 1 tablespoon butter; heat
until sizzling. Add onion and cook, stirring
often, until caramelized, about 10 minutes.
Season to taste with salt and pepper, then add
garlic. Remove from heat. Spread cooked onion
evenly in a 4 x 6-inch baking dish.

Preheat oven to 425° F.

Place squash in a heavy-bottomed saucepan over
medium-high heat and cover with cream, half
and half, bay leaves, thyme, mace, salt, and
pepper. Simmer until squash is tender and has
absorbed most of cream. Remove from heat and

Warm berry compote counterpoints cold orange custard.

discard herb stems and bay leaves. Taste and
adjust seasoning.

Place onions in a lightly greased baking dish,
then layer with squash. Top with Parmesan
cheese and dot with remaining 2 tablespoons
butter. Bake until lightly browned, about 15
minutes. Serve immediately.

Serves 6.

ORANGE CUSTARD WITH WARM COMPOTE OF BERRIES
(Steven Froman, pastry chef)

2 whole eggs
3 egg yolks
Slivered zest of 1 1/2 oranges
2 cups half and half
3/4 cup sugar
1 1/2 tablespoons Grand Marnier
1 cup seedless grapes
1 cup strawberries
1/2 cup raspberries or other berries
Juice of 1/2 orange
Juice of 1/2 lemon
About 2 cups whole strawberries and grapes

Preheat oven to 350° F.

In a bowl, lightly beat whole eggs, yolks, and
zest of 1 orange. In a saucepan, warm half and
half with 1/2 cup sugar. When quite warm, add
slowly to eggs, then add Grand Marnier. Strain
through a fine sieve and pour into individual
ramekins or custard cups. Place in a large pan,
adding hot water about halfway up the side of
the ramekins. Cover the pan and bake until
custard is set, about 30 minutes. Remove from
oven and cool thoroughly.

In a saucepan, combine grapes, strawberries,
raspberries, remaining zest of 1/2 orange, orange
and lemon juices, and remaining 1/4 cup sugar.
Cook over medium heat, stirring continually, for
4 to 5 minutes. Put through a food mill or purée
in a blender or food processor, return to saucepan,
and warm.

Unmold cooled custard and serve with warm
compote poured over and whole berries and
grapes on the side.

Serves 6.

CIAO

CIAO introduced the sleek Italian-moderne look of Milano to San Francisco restaurants when it opened in 1979. The contemporary Italian look coexists here with the old-style Italian relaxed camaraderie of the *trattoria*.

European-born and New York-reared General Manager Barbara Beltaire, who's been in the restaurant business most of her life, finds Ciao to be the most special restaurant she's ever encountered. "It's because the people are so special, both the customers and the staff." She admits to being managed by her staff instead of the other way around. "We're like a big family, with fights and all. Most important to creating a good restaurant is that everyone have fun, customers and personnel alike. Whenever I get customers who're grumpy while waiting for a table, I offer to get them a reservation at another restaurant. We only want people who're here to have a good time."

Ciao's waiters, including a couple of outrageous characters, certainly strive to make diners feel at home. It's the same friendly attitude that prevails at MacArthur Park, Ciao's sister restaurant, just around the corner.

In the midst of all the revelry, Chef Tony Chavez appears very quiet and reserved, turning out festive fare that's heavy on the butter and cream of northern Italy. The evidence here is his green and white *fettuccine* with *pancetta* and cream, and probably the richest chocolate dessert in San Francisco, Cioccolata Valentino.

Buon appetito! Ciao!

Chef Tony Chavez's Menu for Four

Grilled Radicchio
Blanc de Blancs Sparkling Wine,
Proprietors' Selection, Napa Valley, 1980

☐

Paglia e Fieno
Montecarlo Bianco, Fattoria del Teso, 1983

☐

Filetto in Salsa Balsamica
Marcarini Barolo Riserva, 1979

☐

Cioccolata Valentino

OPPOSITE: *General manager Barbara Beltaire (left) and Chef Tony Chavez.* ABOVE: *Sleek Italian design makes Ciao a favorite setting for San Francisco diners.*

Green and white fettuccine with pancetta, peas, and cream.

GRILLED RADICCHIO

(Marinated Italian Lettuce, Charcoal Grilled)

1 cup red wine vinegar
¼ cup extra-virgin olive oil
2 garlic cloves, crushed
Salt
Freshly ground black pepper
2 large heads radicchio, quartered
2 lemons, halved

Prepare coals.

Combine vinegar, oil, garlic, and salt and pepper to taste in a bowl. Dip *radicchio* in mixture and grill over charcoal for about 2 minutes per side. Serve on salad plates with lemon to squeeze over top.

Serves 4.

PAGLIA E FIENO

(Green and White Fettuccine
with Pancetta, Peas, and Cream)

1 pound pancetta or prosciutto, cut into julienne
1 cup (2 sticks) butter
1 pound fresh green peas, shelled
2 cups heavy cream
½ pound each egg and spinach noodles
1 cup freshly grated Parmesan cheese

If using *pancetta,* sauté, and discard grease. Add butter. When butter has melted, add peas and sauté lightly. (If using prosciutto, melt butter and add prosciutto along with peas.) Add cream and cook until slightly reduced.

Meanwhile cook pasta in 4 quarts of boiling salted water until *al dente.* To cream mixture, add drained pasta and Parmesan; toss lightly. Serve immediately.

Serves 4.

FILETTO IN SALSA BALSAMICA

(Grilled Beef Tenderloin with Balsamic Sauce)

1 cup balsamic vinegar
¼ cup olive oil
4 fresh rosemary sprigs
4 teaspoons whole pink pepperberries
Salt
Freshly ground black pepper
8 4-ounce beef tenderloin filets

Prepare coals.

In a saucepan, mix together vinegar, oil, rosemary, pepperberries, and salt and pepper to taste and heat to lukewarm.

In the meantime, sear beef for 30 seconds on each side over charcoal, then grill to desired doneness, turning only once, about 3 to 5 minutes total for rare to 6 to 9 minutes total for well-done. Place beef on serving plates and pour warm sauce over filets. Serve immediately.

Serves 4.

Raspberry sauce embellishes rich chocolate espresso loaf.

Cioccolata Valentino

(Chocolate Espresso Loaf with Raspberry Sauce)

10 amaretti *cookies*
About 1 cup espresso coffee
9 hard-cooked egg yolks
1½ cups (3 sticks) unsalted butter, at room temperature
12 ounces (12 squares) semisweet chocolate, melted
½ cup cocoa
¾ cup canned chocolate fudge topping
2 tablespoons vanilla extract
3 tablespoons brandy
2 tablespoons Amaretto liqueur
6½ ounces (6½ squares) semisweet chocolate, shaved
2 cups fresh raspberries
Sugar

Soak *amaretti* cookies in espresso.

Put egg yolks through a fine sieve into a mixing bowl. Add butter and blend with electric mixer until smooth. Add melted chocolate, cocoa, fudge topping, vanilla, brandy, and Amaretto and beat until light and fluffy, about 10 minutes. Then stir in chocolate shavings.

Line a 9 x 5-inch loaf pan with plastic wrap. Spread one-third of chocolate mixture into bottom of loaf pan. Cover with half of soaked cookies, followed by another layer of chocolate mixture, then remaining cookies, and final layer of chocolate mixture. Freeze for 1½ to 2 hours or longer. Remove from freezer a few minutes before serving, and invert loaf onto a plate or tray.

Reserving a few whole raspberries for garnish, purée berries in a blender or food processor and add sugar to taste; reserve.

To serve, slice loaf into ½-inch-thick pieces. Pour pools of raspberry purée on small plates and top with a slice of chocolate loaf. Garnish with whole raspberries.

Serves 12 to 14.

Fresh pasta and sauces are available to take home.

FOG CITY DINER

YARDS AND YARDS of shiny chrome, black and white glazed tile, flashy neon, shiny black Formica tabletops—all suggestive of the ultimate '50s diner. Add a big noisy crowd, tasty food that's fun to eat, and the best business name to come along in years, and you have one of the hottest spots in San Francisco.

"The Fog City Diner is just plain fun. Everything about it entertains—not because of some loose, party attitude of the owners, but because the restaurant has been put together with such a strong vision. The Fog City Diner is one of those rare places that has done its homework on top of being clever. You know it the minute you see the building and read the menu. Some people are disappointed that the food isn't like it was in the diners and malt shops and chili parlors they grew up with but, frankly, the Fog City Diner is better than any of my memories," drooled *San Francisco Chronicle* critic Patricia Unterman.

Immensely popular since opening in the summer of 1985, Fog City Diner results from the combined talents of three transplanted Chicagoans: Bill Higgins, Bill Upson, and Chef Cindy Pawlcyn. The trio, owners of Real Foods, have also created the popular Mustards in the Napa Valley, and The Rio Grill near Carmel. Californians can thank the blustery weather of a Chicago January for blowing the creators of these original restaurants westward. Back there the trio worked for the restaurant group Lettuce Entertain You; Higgins and Upson as managers of different restaurants and Pawlcyn as sous chef at the Pump Room. Agreeing that the cold there was ridiculous, they began their move to California.

Real Foods' philosophy of food in general "boils down to putting out food that's very good, fresh, simply prepared, and has some imagination. We avoid wild combinations and emphasize fundamental aspects of good American cooking." Fog City also upgrades dishes typical of the diner genre—malts, burgers, chili dogs, apple pie. The menu offers small plates, "American *dim sum*" as Higgins calls them, so diner diners can sample more variety.

Chef-owner Cindy Pawlcyn's Menu for Twelve

Several Salads on a Plate

□

*Grilled Polenta and Sausages
with Fresh Tomato Sauce*

□

Apple Pie or Walnut Torte

OPPOSITE: *Co-owner Bill Higgins (left) with partner-chef Cindy Pawlcyn. ABOVE: Restaurant design glowing with neon idealizes the 1950s.*

The illuminated bar is made of Mexican onyx.

SEVERAL SALADS ON A PLATE

Place the following salads in mounds on a large platter. Serve small amounts of each.

Serves 12, allowing small portions of each.

CURRIED CARROT SALAD

1 tablespoon curry powder
3 garlic cloves, minced
1/3 cup white wine vinegar
Salt
Coarsely ground white pepper
3 tablespoons olive oil
6 medium-sized carrots, peeled and grated

In a small bowl, combine curry powder, garlic, vinegar, and salt and pepper to taste. Let stand 10 minutes for flavors to develop. Whisk in oil. Pour over carrots and mix well.

CUCUMBER SALAD

Salt
6 medium-sized cucumbers, peeled and seeded
3/4 cup sour cream
3 tablespoons minced fresh dill
Coarsely ground white pepper

Salt cucumbers lightly and let stand in a bowl for 30 minutes to 1 hour.

Combine sour cream, dill, and pepper to taste in a bowl. Just before serving, add dressing to cucumbers and mix well.

BEET AND CARROT SALAD

2 tablespoons rice wine vinegar
¼ cup Dijon-style mustard
½ cup olive oil
2 large carrots, peeled and cut into fine julienne
3 large beets, cooked, peeled, and cut into fine julienne

Blend vinegar and mustard, slowly add oil, and
mix well. Add to vegetables and toss thoroughly.

WILD RICE SALAD

4 cups cooked wild rice
1¼ pounds fresh peas, shelled and blanched
2 tablespoons rice wine or champagne vinegar
4 green onions, minced
¼ cup chopped celery hearts and leaves
3 tablespoons olive oil
2 tablespoons virgin olive oil
Salt
Freshly ground black pepper

Combine all ingredients, including seasoning to
taste, and mix well.

GRILLED POLENTA AND SAUSAGES WITH FRESH TOMATO SAUCE

12 cups water
1½ cups (3 sticks) unsalted butter
1½ tablespoons salt
1½ tablespoons ground white pepper
6 cups polenta
½ cup heavy cream
4 cups mixed grated cheeses (Fog City uses Jarlsberg,
    Asiago, and Fontina)
3 eggs, beaten
24 2-ounce sweet Italian sausages
Tomato Sauce (recipe follows)

*Assorted salads on a plate precede or accompany grilled polenta
and sausages with fresh tomato sauce.*

In a deep saucepan over high heat, bring water, butter, salt, and pepper to a full rolling boil. Slowly add *polenta,* stirring constantly; cook, stirring frequently, until thick, about 15 to 20 minutes. Add cream and cheeses; mix. Turn off heat and add eggs. Pour into a bread pan or other deep pan to cool and set. Slice into ½-inch-thick slices.

Prepare coals.

Place sausages on a charcoal grill, turning to cook all sides. When sausages are almost done, place polenta slices on grill to just heat through and crisp outside. (In absence of a charcoal grill, sausages and polenta can be pan-grilled over medium-high heat.)

To serve, arrange 2 to 3 polenta slices in center of each plate with 2 sausages around edges. Top with tomato sauce.

Serves 12.

TOMATO SAUCE

2 shallots, minced
4 tablespoons unsalted butter
4 to 6 peeled, seeded, and diced tomatoes (see note)
Salt
Freshly ground white pepper
¼ cup dry white wine
4 tablespoons minced fresh basil or parsley, or
  combination

Sauté shallots in 2 tablespoons butter until tender, about 5 minutes. Add tomatoes and cook 5 to 8 minutes, adding salt and pepper to taste. Add wine and cook until reduced, about 15 minutes. Beat in remaining 2 tablespoons butter and add herbs. If made ahead, reheat just before serving.

Makes about 3 cups.

NOTE: At Fog City, tomatoes are first slightly smoked by cooking them covered over low coals for 10 to 15 minutes, then they are peeled and seeded.

Offer guests a choice of apple pie or walnut torte.

APPLE PIE

1 cup (2 sticks) unsalted butter
1½ cups powdered sugar
2 egg yolks
1½ cups all-purpose flour
1½ teaspoons freshly grated lemon zest
½ teaspoon vanilla extract
6 to 8 peeled and cored green apples, cut into wedges
¾ cup granulated sugar
Ground cinnamon
Juice of ½ lemon
Unsalted butter
1 egg beaten with 4 tablespoons water
Custard Sauce (recipe follows) or vanilla ice cream

Using two knives held side by side or a pastry blender, combine butter, powdered sugar, egg yolks, flour, lemon zest, and vanilla in a mixing bowl until blended. Add a few drops of ice water if necessary to bind. Wrap in a damp cloth or plastic film and chill.

Preheat oven to 350° F.

Roll pastry to a 14-inch circle and place on a large baking sheet.

Mound apples on pastry, leaving a 2½- to 3-inch border. Sprinkle apples with sugar, cinnamon to taste, and lemon juice. Dot liberally with butter.

Brush edges of pastry around apples with egg wash. Beginning with a small section, fold pastry up around apples and brush outside edge with egg mixture. Fold up the next section and continue around apples, pressing slightly overlapping sections of dough together. Bake until golden, about 55 to 60 minutes. Serve wedges with Custard Sauce or vanilla ice cream.

Serves 10 to 12.

CUSTARD SAUCE

2½ cups heavy cream
¾ cup milk
8 egg yolks
¾ cup sugar
2 teaspoons vanilla extract
Bourbon

Heat cream and milk in a small saucepan over medium heat just until hot; reduce heat to low and simmer 10 minutes. In top of a double boiler set over barely simmering water, whisk egg yolks and sugar until light and lemon colored. Beat hot milk gradually into yolk mixture. Cook, stirring constantly, until thick enough to coat a metal spoon, about 10 minutes. Remove from heat and add vanilla and bourbon to taste. Serve hot, warm, or cold.

Makes about 4 cups.

WALNUT TORTE

4 eggs, separated
1 cup sugar
1 cup finely ground walnuts
½ cup all-purpose flour
1 teaspoon baking powder
½ cup (1 stick) plus 3 tablespoons butter,
  melted and cooled
1 tablespoon vanilla extract
½ teaspoon almond extract
Powdered sugar (for dusting)
Chocolate sauce (use your favorite recipe), warmed

Beat egg yolks with ½ cup sugar. Mix ground walnuts with ¼ cup of remaining sugar. Mix flour with baking powder and fold it alternately with walnut mixture into egg yolk mixture. Add butter and vanilla and almond extracts. Beat egg whites with remaining ¼ cup sugar until stiff but not dry. Fold into egg-walnut mixture. Pour into a lightly buttered and floured 8-inch springform pan. Place in a cold oven. Turn heat to 300° F. Bake until springy but still moist in center, about 30 to 40 minutes. Dust with powdered sugar and serve with warm chocolate sauce.

Serves 8 to 12.

GAYLORD INDIA RESTAURANT

GAYLORD introduced a new form of grilling to San Francisco when it opened in 1976. Until then authentic *tandoori* cooking was illegal in California due to the intense heat of the ovens. In fact, the heat is so infernal that the ovens must be replaced about every two years.

In all there are eleven Gaylord satellites of the New Delhi original, although the San Francisco branch, owned by the Ajanta Corporation (which operates four in North America), is acknowledged among critics as serving the best Indian food this side of New Delhi. The elegant and comfortable dining room also offers one of the City's most picturesque views of the bay. Lush tropical plants add a cooling effect, and Indian paintings and sculpture add authenticity.

In spite of its Ghirardelli Square location, a major tourist attraction, Gaylord has a large local following. Less than 30 percent of their diners are out-of-towners, according to General Manager Pushpraj Goswami.

Chef Peshori Lal has been with Gaylord's for over twenty-five years, starting in New Dehli, then moving to the Chicago branch before transferring to San Francisco. The rest of his exclusively Indian kitchen staff speak no English, therefore the waiters are all bilingual.

Gaylord's bar is unique in this collection of bar & grills. British and American cocktails, California wines, Indian beers, and yogurt refreshers are served on carved coffee tables. The comfortably cushioned banquettes are upholstered in a black, gold, and magenta fabric patterned in an Indian motif.

Chef Peshori Lal's Menu for Four

Lassi

□

Dal Soup

□

Tandoori Murg

Shahi Korma

Kashmiri Pillau

Aloo Gobi

Taj Mahal Beer (India) or J. Lohr Petite Sirah

□

Kheer

OPPOSITE: *Exotic drinks and Indian beer in Gaylord's bar.* ABOVE: *Indian feast includes (clockwise from foreground), dal soup, silver-coated bread (recipe not included), potatoes and cauliflower, curried lamb, tandoori chicken, and rice pilaf.*

Diners enjoy splendid views of the Bay.

LASSI

(Yogurt Drink)

2 cups plain yogurt
2 cups cold water
Sugar
Rosewater
Ice

In a blender, combine yogurt and water with sugar and rosewater to taste; blend until smooth. Serve in tall glasses over ice.

Serves 4.

DAL SOUP

(Lentil Soup)

¼ pound moong lentils (see note)
6 cups water
½-inch piece fresh ginger root, chopped
2 large garlic cloves, minced
½ teaspoon ground turmeric
½ teaspoon cayenne pepper
2 teaspoons paprika
Salt
½ cup heavy cream
Juice of 1 lemon

Wash lentils in several changes of standing water until water turns clear. Cook lentils in 5 cups water over high heat. Bring to boil and remove and discard any foam with a slotted spoon. Add 1 cup water, ginger, garlic, turmeric, cayenne, paprika, and salt to taste. Reduce heat to medium and cook until lentils turn mushy, about 45 minutes. Strain through a sieve into a saucepan, place over low heat, add cream and lemon juice, and heat; do not allow to boil.

Serves 4.

NOTE: *Moong* lentils and Indian spices are available at East Indian stores, specialty gourmet shops, or by mail order from India Foods & Gifts, 643 Post, SF 94109.

TANDOORI MURG

(Spiced Roast Chicken)

1 3-pound chicken
6 garlic cloves
1 1-inch piece fresh ginger root, peeled
1 cup plain yogurt
Juice of 1 lemon
1 teaspoon salt
1 teaspoon cayenne pepper (optional)

1 tablespoon paprika
1 teaspoon ground cumin
About ½ cup (1 stick) melted butter
Lemon wedges (garnish)
Thinly sliced red onion (garnish)

Disjoint chicken into 4 pieces, discarding wings and rib cage. Remove fat and skin from chicken. With a sharp knife, cut 3 vertical slashes into each piece of chicken.

Chop garlic and ginger in a blender or food processor; add yogurt, lemon juice, salt, cayenne, paprika, and cumin, and blend into a paste. Rub paste into chicken and marinate overnight in a covered dish in the refrigerator. Return chicken to room temperature before cooking.

Preheat oven to highest temperature.

Place chicken on a rack in a baking dish and cook in oven for 10 minutes. Baste chicken with melted butter. Reduce heat to 325° F and cook until chicken pieces are tender when pierced and juices run clear, about 20 minutes. Garnish with lemon wedges and sliced onion.

Serves 4.

SHAHI KORMA

(Curried Lamb)

6 tablespoons vegetable oil
1 large onion, sliced
1 tablespoon ground cumin
8 to 10 whole green cardamom pods, gently crushed (see note under Dal Soup)
2 cinnamon sticks
1½ pounds lean lamb, cut into ½-inch cubes
1 1-inch piece fresh ginger root, peeled and minced
4 garlic cloves, minced
¾ cup plain yogurt
1 quart milk
1 teaspoon ground turmeric
1 teaspoon cayenne pepper
Salt

¾ cup heavy cream
¼ cup sliced almonds
½ cup raw cashews, ground into a paste
2 tablespoons chopped fresh cilantro (garnish)
2 hard-cooked eggs, grated (garnish)

Heat oil in a sauté pan or skillet over medium-high heat. Add onion, cumin, cardamom, and cinnamon and cook until onion turns light brown, about 10 minutes.

Wash lamb under running hot water until meat assumes a glassy shine.

To onion mixture, add lamb, ginger, garlic, yogurt, milk, turmeric, cayenne, and salt to taste. Cook over high heat for about 25 minutes, stirring constantly to prevent milk from scalding. Reduce heat and add cream, almonds, and cashew paste. Cover skillet and cook until lamb is tender, about 25 minutes. Remove cinnamon sticks before serving.

Serve garnished with cilantro and egg.

Serves 4.

KASHMIRI PILLAU

(Rice Pilaf)

4 tablespoons vegetable oil
1 garlic clove, minced
1 1-inch piece fresh ginger root, peeled and minced
1 teaspoon ground cumin
1 cinnamon stick
6 whole green cardamom pods (see note under Dal Soup)
6 cups cold water
¾ tablespoons salt
3 cups long-grain rice, preferably basmati
1 pinch saffron soaked in ½ cup hot water
Golden raisins (garnish)
Raw cashews (garnish)

Preheat oven to 350° F.

Heat oil in heavy pot over medium-high heat, add ginger, garlic, cumin, cinnamon, and cardamom, and cook until garlic browns, about 3 to 5 minutes. Add cold water and salt. While water comes to a full boil, wash rice in several changes of standing water until water becomes clear, then add rice to boiling water. After about 80 percent of the water has evaporated, add saffron-infused water and mix into rice. Place a damp cloth towel or cheesecloth directly on rice and cover pot with a weighted lid. Place pot in oven for 10 minutes.

Serve hot, garnished with raisins and cashews.

Serves 4 to 6.

ALOO GOBI

(Potatoes and Cauliflower)

5 tablespoons vegetable oil
½ teaspoon ground cumin
1 1-inch piece fresh ginger root, peeled and chopped
3 garlic cloves, chopped
3 medium-sized tomatoes, peeled, seeded, and chopped
1 teaspoon ground turmeric
1 teaspoon cayenne pepper
1 teaspoon salt
3 medium-sized potatoes, peeled and cut into
    6 pieces each
1 head cauliflower, broken or cut into bite-sized pieces
Chopped fresh cilantro (garnish)

Heat oil in a sauté pan or skillet over medium-high heat, add cumin, ginger, and garlic, and cook until garlic is lightly browned, about 3 to 5 minutes. Add tomatoes, turmeric, cayenne, and salt, reduce heat to medium-low, and cook until thickened into a paste, about 25 to 35 minutes. Add potatoes and cauliflower. Cover pan, reduce heat to low, and cook until vegetables are tender, about 20 to 25 minutes. Garnish with cilantro.

Serves 4.

KHEER

(Rice Pudding)

½ gallon extra-rich milk
½ cup long-grain rice
3 tablespoons sugar
1 tablespoon raisins
1 tablespoon slivered blanched almonds

Place milk in a heavy pot over high heat, constantly stirring to prevent milk from scorching or boiling over. When milk boils, add rice and return to a boil. Remove from heat for 1 minute without stirring. Place milk over medium heat, stirring constantly until rice is cooked, about 30 minutes. Stir in sugar, raisins, and almonds. Remove from heat and serve either hot or cold.

Serves 4.

Manager Kishore Kripalani (left) and chef Peshori Lal.

HARRIS'

NATIVE TEXAN Ann Harris is the perfect hostess. Her natural hospitality was polished in 1977 when she and her late husband Jack opened a successful ranch-kitchen coffee shop and a Mexican-influenced dining room on the Harris Ranch along Interstate 5 towards Los Angeles. When her husband died, it seemed time for a new project. Steve Tumbas of Café Bedford, who'd worked at the ranch restaurants, suggested that she open a quality steakhouse in San Francisco. Upon learning that Grisson's, a fifty-year-old steakery, was for sale, she looked no farther. The next year and, obviously, a large sum of money was spent in totally redoing the low-ceilinged, dark space that had originally been an automobile showroom.

In designing her restaurant, Ann Harris was determined to move against the tide of noisy rooms, opting for a place where people could feel comfortable. The result is a conservatively luxurious bar and restaurant in the style of an Old–San Francisco men's clubhouse. Pacific Union, Bohemian Club, and Family Club members should feel at home here, as will anyone who enjoys comfort.

In addition to the clublike dining room, guests may dine in small, intimate rooms that capture the early San Francisco restaurant tradition of privacy, including a library with four tables near a fireplace.

Goetz Boje has worked with Mrs. Harris since the beginning of the Harris Ranch restaurant. German-born, European-trained, and apprenticed in major Swiss, German, and London hotels, Boje's first work in San Francisco was in private clubs and hotels including the Hilton. He was cooking at MacArthur Park when Jean Harris discovered him. She also took Joey Buhagiar from MacArthur Park to the Harris Ranch; he now manages the San Francisco Harris'.

Harris' philosophy? "Simple elegance, no frills, everything in the best of taste. I want people to dine, not just eat," sums up Mrs. Harris.

Reminiscent of the Harris Ranch packing house days, sides of hard-to-find Prime beef hang in a streetside showcase window for only one day, then get cut for use in the kitchen or sold at a take-out meat market counter. Almost all parts of the cow appear on the restaurant menu. Sweetbreads and brains, simply sauteed in butter with a bit of lemon juice, are specialties, and mountain oysters are available on request. Non-meat-eaters can opt for the grilled or poached catch of the day.

Chef Goetz Boje's Menu for Six

Harris' Country Pâté
Château St. Jean Chardonnay, Robert Young

□

Cold Cucumber Soup

□

Roast Filet of Beef with Madeira Sauce
Bouquet of Fresh Vegetables
Potato Shells
Jordan Cabernet Sauvignon, Alexander, 1980

□

Cognac Mousse

ABOVE: Roast filet of beef with Madeira sauce is accompanied by crisply cooked vegetables.

HARRIS' COUNTRY PÂTÉ

2 pounds sweetbreads
Juice of 1 lemon
1 cup canned jellied consommé
1/2 pound braunschweiger
1/2 cup heavy cream
1/2 cup dry sherry
3 tablespoons brandy
1/2 cup chopped pitted black olives
1/4 cup chopped unsalted pistachio nuts
1/2 cup (1 stick) soft butter
1/4 teaspoon ground nutmeg
Pinch of ground mace
Salt
Ground white pepper

Cover sweetbreads in cold water and refrigerate for several hours.

Drain sweetbreads and place in a saucepan with lemon juice in water to cover; bring to a boil and simmer until tender, about 5 minutes. Drain and rinse under cold water. Remove and discard membranes and chill sweetbreads.

Place sweetbreads in a blender or food processor and blend with consommé. Add remaining ingredients, including salt and pepper to taste, and blend until smooth. Pack in small serving crocks. Serve with melba toasts for spreading.

Serves 6 to 8.

Murals depict pastoral scenes from the Harris Ranch.

COLD CUCUMBER SOUP

¼ cup minced onion
2 tablespoons butter
2 medium-sized cucumbers, peeled, seeded, and cubed
1½ cups homemade chicken stock or canned
  low-sodium broth
1½ cups buttermilk
½ teaspoon salt, or to taste
½ teaspoon ground white pepper
2 tablespoons chopped fresh dill
½ teaspoon curry (optional)
3 teaspoons sour cream
6 fresh dill, watercress, or parsley sprigs (garnish)

Sauté onion in butter in a small pan over medium heat until onion is soft, about 10 minutes. Place in a blender or food processor and add cucumbers, stock, buttermilk, salt, pepper, chopped dill, and curry; purée until smooth. Chill, covered, for 4 hours.

Serve very cold in chilled bowls. Garnish each bowl with ½ teaspoon sour cream and a sprig of herb.

Serves 6.

Chef Goetz Boje.

ROAST FILET OF BEEF WITH MADEIRA SAUCE

1 whole beef filet, all fat and sinew removed (about
  5 pounds trimmed), at room temperature (see note)
2 tablespoons flour
1 cup canned beef bouillon (not consommé)
Salt
Freshly ground black pepper
Worcestershire sauce
Grated lemon zest
¼ cup plus 2 tablespoons Madeira or dry sherry
1 tablespoon butter
Chopped fresh parsley (garnish)

Preheat oven to 500° F.

Place meat on a rack in a roasting pan rubbed with butter; do not cover. Immediately turn oven down to 350° F and roast meat until internal temperature reaches 120° F for rare, approximately 30 minutes. Remove from oven and keep warm.

To make Madeira sauce, pour off fat from roasting pan, reserving 2 tablespoons in a saucepan. Add flour to saucepan and cook over medium-high heat until well blended. Add bouillon and simmer until thickened, about 5 minutes. Add salt and pepper to taste, a dash or Worcestershire, and a touch of grated lemon zest. Reserve.

Add ¼ cup Madeira or sherry to the roasting pan and deglaze, scraping the bottom of the roasting pan, and place over low heat until slightly reduced. Strain and return to pan. Add reserved bouillon mixture and continue to cook for about 10 minutes. When ready to serve, add 2 tablespoons Madeira or sherry and 1 tablespoon butter and swirl gently into the sauce until melted.

Slice beef approximately ¾ inch thick and serve with Madeira sauce. Garnish with parsley.

Serves 6 to 8.

NOTE: You may wish to remove the tail end of filet and reserve it for another use; otherwise double it under to equalize thickness of the whole portion.

POTATO SHELLS

6 russet potatoes, scrubbed and dried
Vegetable oil
Butter

Preheat oven to 400° F.

Rub potatoes with oil and bake until soft when pierced, about 40 to 60 minutes depending upon size. Cut in half lengthwise and remove as much potato as possible, leaving only a thin layer of potato inside skin. Cut each half lengthwise into 2 wedges, spread with a little butter, and place under a hot broiler for a few minutes until brown.

Serves 6.

Harris' also features a take-out market for prime beef.

COGNAC MOUSSE

(Jean-Ives Charon, pastry chef)

1 cup sugar
½ cup water
¼ cup milk
4 egg yolks
½ cup cognac
1 9-inch-round chocolate sponge cake (use any
*   good recipe)*
2 envelopes (2 tablespoons or ½ ounce) plain gelatin
1 tablespoon cold water
1 tablespoon boiling water
1½ cups egg whites (about 12 large eggs)
1½ cups heavy cream
Shaved chocolate curls (garnish)

Make a simple syrup by combining ½ cup sugar and ½ cup water in a saucepan over high heat and boil until sugar is melted and mixture reaches syrup consistency. Cool and reserve.

Place hot water in bottom half of a double boiler, making sure water does not touch bottom of top pan. Bring to a boil over high heat, then reduce heat so water barely simmers. Heat milk to scalding (approximately 180° F) in top pan set over simmering water. In a bowl, beat egg yolks with remaining ½ cup sugar until well mixed and lemon-colored, about 4 minutes with an electric mixer. Whisk egg yolks gradually into hot milk and cook over simmering water until custard coats a metal spoon, about 10 minutes. Remove from heat and add ¼ cup cognac. Set aside.

Line a 9-inch round cake pan with baking parchment. Make a collar of parchment around pan approximately 4 inches high. Place sponge cake in bottom of pan.

Add remaining ¼ cup cognac to ¼ cup simple syrup and pour over cake to soak.

Soften gelatin in cold water for about 1 minute, then add boiling water and stir until dissolved. Reserve.

Beat egg whites to soft peak stage. Lightly whip cream. Fold egg whites into custard mixture, then fold in whipped cream and dissolved gelatin. Pour mixture over cake. Chill at least 4 hours before removing collar. Garnish with chocolate curls before serving.

ALTERNATIVE: For individual desserts as shown in photograph, cut circles from sponge cake to fit eight 3-inch individual soufflé dishes lined and collared with baking parchment. Distribute cream mixture evenly among dishes and chill as directed above. Prepare Crème Anglaise or a thin custard sauce, made from a favorite recipe, and pour in individual plates. Remove cakes from dishes and place on center of each plate. Spoon additional custard over cake. Drizzle custard with melted semisweet chocolate and draw a knife through sauce to form a pattern.

Serves 8.

Individual cognac mousse.

Carved wooden bar adds to the clubhouse atmosphere.

HAYES STREET GRILL

*A*H, HERE'S MY CHANCE to write a critique of the restaurant owned by the premier food critic of the City! But this isn't a book of reviews, and if it were, I'd have mostly accolades for Patricia Unterman, and her partners Ann Powning Haskel, Robert Flaherty, and Richard Sander, owners of Hayes Street Grill. So what if I find the *pommes frites* no longer the sublime morsels they were when the restaurant opened in 1979; maybe I caught the kitchen on a couple of off-nights. The grilled fish and nightly specials remain as first-rate as ever, and the Crème Brûlée recipe shared here is the best version I've ever eaten.

Obviously inspired by the simple decor and style of the historic Sam's and Tadich grills, Hayes Street Grill puts emphasis on its food. The insistence on freshness is implied even in the last-minute, hand-written menu on the blackboard.

Known primarily for moist grilled fish with a choice of simple sauces, Hayes Street Grill is *San Francisco Focus* magazine readers' choice for best seafood in the Bay Area. Additionally, the succulent housemade sausages, innovative salads and desserts, and an affordable collection of superb California wines give Hayes Street a large following. In fact, it usually makes almost everyone's list of favorite San Francisco eateries.

Unterman studied cooking with Josephine Araldo, writes a weekly restaurant column for the *San Francisco Chronicle,* co-authored *Restaurants of San Francisco* (Chronicle Books), and was named to Who's Cooking in America by *The Cook's Magazine.* She was co-owner of the Beggar's Banquet, a vegetarian-style restaurant in Berkeley where she met her present partners. Together they germinated the idea for a grill in the San Francisco Civic Center and performing arts area. Hayes Street Grill was the first quality restaurant to open in the rundown neighborhood, leading the way for a continuing rejuvenation.

Haskel, who studied cooking in France and worked in French charcuteries, and Unterman are responsible for the kitchen. Flaherty, a reformed lawyer, and Sander, a former East Bay educator, handle the business, purchasing, and staff.

Owner Patricia Unterman's Menu for Six

Green Salad with Smoked Trout Toasts

☐

Portuguese-style Steamed Clams

*Torres Gran Coronas Reserva
or a light Rhône red or Tuscany red*

☐

Crème Brûlée

ABOVE: Clams are steamed in a flavorful broth seasoned with garlic, red sweet peppers, tomatoes, and spicy Portuguese-style sausage.

Photos of celebrated patrons line the walls.

Genial host Alan Zimmerman "is the Hayes Street Grill to most people," according to owner Patricia Unterman.

GREEN SALAD WITH SMOKED TROUT TOASTS

½ cup homemade mayonnaise
¾ cup crumbled boned smoked trout
2 tablespoons snipped fresh chives
Freshly squeezed lemon juice
1 French-style baguette, cut into 18 slices
About 6 cups mixed young lettuces, washed, dried, and chilled
Vinaigrette (use your favorite recipe)

In a small bowl, combine mayonnaise and trout, mashing them together with a fork. Stir in chives and a little lemon juice to taste. Cover and refrigerate overnight.

Spread baguette slices on a baking sheet and place in a 250° F oven until golden and crisp. If made ahead, cool and store in an airtight container. Just before serving, spread smoked trout mixture on toasts.

Toss lettuces with vinaigrette and serve with toasts.

Serves 6.

PORTUGUESE-STYLE STEAMED CLAMS

1 tablespoon minced garlic, more or less according to taste
2 cups chopped onions
3 cups chopped red sweet pepper
½ pound high-quality chorizo or Italian pork sausage, crumbled
⅓ cup olive oil
1½ cups dry white wine
6 cups well-flavored homemade fish or chicken stock, or canned low-sodium chicken broth
Dried red pepper flakes
2 cups peeled, seeded, and chopped flavorful ripe tomatoes (optional)
60 to 72 small to medium-sized clams, well scrubbed
Chopped fresh parsley, preferably flat-leaf Italian type, or cilantro

In large sauté pan or skillet, sauté garlic, onions, red pepper, and sausage in olive oil until sausage is cooked, about 12 to 15 minutes. Add wine to mixture and deglaze pan, scraping the bottom of the pan. Add fish or chicken stock and cook until mixture is partly reduced and has a full, rich flavor. Using a slotted spoon, skim off any fat that has risen to surface. Add pepper flakes to taste and chopped tomato. (This can be done ahead and refrigerated until just before serving time.)

About 15 minutes before serving, heat broth to boiling, add clams, cover, and cook until clams have opened, about 6 to 10 minutes. Ladle into individual bowls and garnish with parsley. Serve with tasty bread, with a spoon for broth and a fork for clams.

Serves 6.

CRÈME BRÛLÉE

8 egg yolks
5 tablespoons plus 1 teaspoon sugar
3 cups heavy cream, heated
Brown sugar

Preheat oven to 250° F.

Beat egg yolks with sugar, gradually add hot cream, and pour mixture into individual custard cups. Place in an ovenproof pan, add boiling water to halfway up custard cups, and bake until custards are set and a knife inserted in the center comes out clean, about 50 to 60 minutes. Remove from oven, cool, and chill.

Preheat broiler.

Sprinkle tops with a thin layer of brown sugar. Using a mister, spray sugar with a little water. Place under preheated broiler until sugar melts and tops are bubbly, about 1 minute. Chill before serving.

Serves 6 to 8.

Menus are handwritten daily and displayed over the open kitchen.

L'Entrecôte de Paris

A GLASS-ENCLOSED extension of L'Entrecôte de Paris' original interior creates the feeling of a sidewalk cafe, with vine-covered trellises surrounding windows that open onto the street. In the evening candles and art deco lamps cast a soft glow on Erté high-fashion posters. The white, pink, and black color scheme and recorded music suggest Paris. Only the towering palm tree, which appears to grow through the roof but which the extension actually has been built around, reminds you that you're in California instead of France.

Alexander Mortazavi is proud of the fact that his French-style grill is the only restaurant in America licensed to use the secret shallot-butter-herb sauce that's served with grilled *entrecôte* at the Parisian bistro of the same name. There only *entrecôte,* a thin cut of steak, is served, but the San Francisco variation offers a complete menu including grilled California fare, even the ubiquitous California burger, teamed with classic *pommes frites.*

This is the only restaurant I encountered without a chef in evidence. Instead, the recipes are Mortazavi's, and he credits his entire *brigade de cuisine* with the dishes that come out of his kitchen.

At the last minute I had second thoughts about including L'Entrecôte de Paris in this collection. Although the food is good, the service very friendly, the host congenial, and the setting interesting, the restaurant is a little threadbare around the edges. I hope by the time the book is printed, the walls will have seen a fresh coat of paint, the flowers will be better maintained, and the chipped dishes will be replaced.

Owner Alexander Mortazavi's Menu for Four

Framboise Royal

□

Epinard à la Crêpe de Fromage Chaude

Beaujolais Jadot, Louis Jadot

□

Moules Glacées au Parmesan

□

Canard aux Framboises

Cru Bourgeois du Medoc,
Château La Tour de By, 1983

□

La Tarte Tatin

OPPOSITE: *Glassed extension along the Union Street sidewalk adds to the Parisian flavor.* ABOVE: *Warm goat cheese crepes served on a bed of spinach and drizzled with vinaigrette.*

FRAMBOISE ROYAL

1 bottle champagne, preferably Philippe de Bourgogne,
    chilled
Framboise liqueur

Pour champagne into 4 fluted glasses and add
Framboise to taste.

Serves 4.

EPINARD À LA CRÊPE
DE FROMAGE CHAUDE
(Warm Cheese Crepe on Spinach
with Hearts of Palm)

8 thin slices Brie or blue cheese, at room temperature
8 very thin crepes (use your favorite recipe)
Fresh spinach leaves
1 carrot, cut into julienne
8 canned hearts of palm, cut into 2-inch pieces
4 cherry tomatoes
12 black olives
Vinaigrette (use your favorite recipe)
1/4 cup minced walnuts

Lay a slice of cheese on each crepe and fold over
ends and sides to form a rectangular-shaped
package. Heat in a microwave just until cheese
melts and crepes are hot, about 45 seconds.
(Or heat in a preheated 350° F oven for about
5 minutes.)

Arrange spinach in a rosette pattern on individual
salad plates and top each with 2 warm crepes.
Garnish with carrot, hearts of palm, cherry
tomatoes, and black olives. Drizzle crepes and
vegetables with vinaigrette, then sprinkle with
walnuts.

Serves 4.

*Parmesan cheese is sprinkled over mussels before glazing under
the broiler.*

MOULES GLACÉES AU PARMESAN

(Glazed Mussels with Parmesan Cheese)

24 small mussels, beards removed, well scrubbed with
* a wire brush*
½ cup freshly grated Parmesan cheese
2 tablespoons butter
Juice of 1 lemon
¼ cup minced fresh parsley
1 head firm lettuce, shredded
Lemon wedges

Steam or boil mussels in plain water just until
they open. Remove and discard top shell. Place
mussels-on-the-half-shell on a pan and sprinkle
about 1 teaspoon Parmesan on each.

Preheat broiler.

Bring butter and lemon juice to boil in a small
saucepan and drizzle over mussels. Sprinkle with
parsley and place under broiler until mussels are
hot and cheese is lightly browned. To serve,
arrange 6 mussels on each of 4 plates covered
with shredded lettuce. Garnish with lemon
wedges.

Serves 4.

Owner Alexander Mortazavi.

CANARD AUX FRAMBOISES

(Duck with Raspberry Sauce)

2 ducks (about 4 pounds each)
4 celery stalks, chopped
2 carrots, chopped
Salt
Freshly ground black pepper
2 tablespoons sugar
2 tablespoons dry red wine
Juice of 2 lemons
2 cups fresh raspberries, puréed
4 small spinach leaves (garnish)
4 tomato roses, made from tomato peelings (garnish)

Remove breast meat and legs (leaving thighs)
from ducks and reserve. Place remainder of
ducks in a stockpot with water to cover; add
celery, carrots, and salt and pepper to taste.
Bring to a boil over moderately high heat and
continue boiling until partly reduced, about
1 hour. Strain broth and discard remainder. Boil
broth in saucepan over high heat until reduced
by half. Reserve.

Prepare coals or preheat broiler.

Combine sugar, wine, and lemon juice in a sauté
pan or skillet over medium heat and boil until
sugar is melted and caramelized, about 5 minutes. Add raspberries and 2 cups reduced broth;
cook over low heat until slightly thick, about
15 minutes. Season to taste with salt and pepper.

Season duck pieces to taste with salt and pepper
and grill over medium-hot charcoal. Sear directly
over coals for about 2 minutes per side, then
place over indirect heat, cover grill, and cook,
turning once, until skin is crisp but breast meat
remains pink inside, about 10 minutes per side.
(In absence of a charcoal grill, duck can be cooked
under a preheated broiler.) Slice breast thinly
and arrange on each plate in a fan shape. Place a
leg in center and pour sauce over duck. Garnish
each plate with a spinach leaf and a tomato rose.

Serves 4.

LA TARTE TATIN

(Upside-down Caramelized Apple Tart)

14 red Rome or other good baking apples
1 cup (2 sticks) unsalted butter, cut into 1-inch pieces
2¼ cups sugar
Pastry dough (use your favorite recipe)

Peel apples, core, and cut in half vertically. Cover
bottom of a heavy-bottomed 10-inch ovenproof
skillet with butter, sprinkle with sugar until
evenly coated, and top with apple halves, standing upright. Cover with a second 10-inch ovenproof skillet and place over low heat for 20
minutes. Remove top skillet, increase heat to
medium, and cook until sugar and butter are
caramelized and apples start to brown, about
15 minutes. Remove skillet from heat, allow to
cool, then refrigerate until caramel hardens,
about 2 hours.

Preheat oven to 400° F.

Roll pastry dough into a circle that will just
touch edges of skillet. Using fingers, press down
dough to fit tightly over apples. Prick pastry
with a fork and bake until golden brown, about
45 minutes. Cool, then refrigerate for 2 hours.

Place skillet over high heat and shake until
caramelized apples separate from bottom of pan,
about 1 to 2 minutes. Cover with a plate or other
flat surface and invert. Serve at room temperature
or heated, plain or with whipped cream or
vanilla ice cream.

Serves 12.

MacArthur Park

*T*OUTED FOR THE BEST barbecued baby back ribs in town, MacArthur Park is the flagship restaurant in a successful string of unique establishments opened by Spectrum Foods under the direction of Jerry Magnin, son of Cyril, the San Francisco retail magnate.

It was MacArthur Park's fresh new look of exposed-brick walls, skylights, and huge indoor trees that gave the design world the "woodsy-bricksy fern bar" image associated with San Francisco interiors of the early 1970s. Recent ownership changes (Spectrum was sold to Saga Foods) and a refurbished decor under the direction of General Manager Danny Sullivan have done little to change the formula of this spot that's remained popular since opening day in 1972.

Friday night's end-of-the-work-week crowd still packs the place brick wall to brick wall, and the long lines of $100,000-a-year yuppies waiting to heap their plates with free appetizers is reminiscent of a cattle call.

Chef Ed Kaskey's selections here from MacArthur Park's regular menu are highlighted by spicy crayfish sausages served with an oyster and fresh chili sauce. Unfortunately, crayfish were out of season when we photographed, and the chef's integrity for using only the freshest ingredients wouldn't let him fake it for the camera. Bravo!

Chef Ed Kasky's Menu for Six

Grilled Escarole, Smoked Ham,
and Goat Cheese Appetizer

□

Sizzling Crayfish Sausage
with Smoked Oyster and Pasilla Sauce

Cakebread Sauvignon Blanc, 1984

□

Cobb Salad MacArthur Park

□

Grilled Duck Breast
with Braised Red Cabbage and Smoked Bacon

Duckhorn Merlot, 1983
or Acacia West Vineyard Pinot Noir, 1981

□

Strawberry Shortcake

ABOVE: Off-hours scene of MacArthur Park's bar that teems with patrons in the evening.

Chef Ed Kasky and general manager Danny Sullivan.

Prepare coals or preheat broiler.

Spread about a tablespoon of cheese onto center of each piece of ham, then lay 2 escarole leaves over cheese and dribble a little dressing over filling. Roll up like a jelly roll, with ham on outside. Secure with a toothpick. Dip ends of each ham roll in dressing and grill over a slow charcoal fire or under a preheated broiler until heated through, about 3 to 5 minutes.

To serve, remove toothpicks and place 2 ham rolls per person on a serving plate and spoon some remaining dressing over top.

Serves 6.

GRILLED ESCAROLE, SMOKED HAM, AND GOAT CHEESE APPETIZER

3 tablespoons white wine vinegar
3 tablespoons freshly squeezed orange juice
2 tablespoons stone-ground mustard
¼ teaspoon salt
¼ teaspoon cracked black pepper
⅔ cup olive oil
6 ounces creamy goat cheese
12 boneless smoked ham slices, 1/16 inch thick x
*   5 inches square*
24 escarole leaves, washed and dried

To make dressing, combine vinegar, orange juice, mustard, salt, and pepper in a small bowl or jar. Add olive oil, whisking to combine. Reserve.

SIZZLING CRAYFISH SAUSAGE

1 pound salmon fillets, roughly chopped
8 ounces scallops
12 ounces fresh large prawns, peeled and deveined
2 eggs
1¾ cups heavy cream
1 pound cooked crayfish meat (approximately 5 pounds
*   peeled whole crayfish)*
3 fresh Fresno chilies, seeded and minced
2 fresh poblano chilies, seeded and minced
2 tablespoons minced fresh cilantro leaves
1 garlic clove, minced
1 tablespoon salt
Sheep casing
3 tablespoons butter
4 garlic cloves, mashed
3 tablespoons grated fresh horseradish root
1 large head escarole, green tops removed and each leaf
*   cut in half lengthwise*
Juice of 2 large lemons
Salt
Freshly ground black pepper
Smoked Oyster and Pasilla Sauce (recipe follows)

MacArthur Park popularized the exposed brick, plant-filled decor of the early 1970s.

Blend salmon, scallops, 8 ounces prawns, eggs, and cream in a blender or food processor until smooth.

Dice crayfish and remaining prawns and stir them into blended mixture along with chilies, cilantro, garlic, and salt.

With a sausage-stuffing cone, stuff sheep casing with mixture and tie off links with cotton string to desired length.

Prepare coals.

Steam sausage for 3 minutes before grilling over hardwood charcoal and sage cuttings, turning occasionally, until browned and cooked through, about 4 minutes.

In a large sauté pan or skillet, melt butter over medium heat. Add garlic and horseradish and cook for 3 minutes. Add escarole and cook until escarole is soft but still slightly crisp. Add lemon juice along with salt and pepper to taste.

Serve sausages over escarole with Smoked Oyster and Pasilla Sauce.

Serves 6; allow 4 small links per serving.

Rows of blue cheese, bacon, chicken, tomato and egg top Cobb salad.

SMOKED OYSTER AND PASILLA SAUCE

1 tablespoon butter
½ cup minced seeded fresh pasilla *chilies (about 2 large chilies)*
1 quart heavy cream
¾ cup fresh smoked oysters or canned if fresh are unavailable
¼ cup homemade beef stock or canned low-sodium broth
Salt
Freshly ground black pepper

In a saucepan, melt butter and add chilies. Cook over medium heat until chilies are soft, about 5 minutes. Add cream and reduce by half or until thick.

In a blender or food processor, blend oysters and broth until smooth. Add this to mixture in saucepan and simmer for 10 minutes. Add salt and pepper to taste. (If sauce becomes too thick add a little milk.)

Makes about 3 cups.

COBB SALAD MACARTHUR PARK

1 head romaine lettuce, washed, dried, and torn into bite-sized pieces
1 head iceberg lettuce, washed, dried, and torn into bite-sized pieces
Olive oil
Vinegar
Salt
Freshly ground black pepper
1 cup diced cooked chicken breast
1 cup crumbled smoked bacon
1 cup grated hard-cooked eggs
1 cup crumbled Roquefort cheese
1 cup diced tomatoes
1½ avocados, peeled, quartered, and partially sliced through

Toss lettuces to taste with oil, vinegar, salt, and pepper. Distribute them evenly in 6 individual bowls and arrange other ingredients in separate rows on top. Place fanned-out avocado slices in center of each salad.

Serves 6.

GRILLED DUCK BREAST WITH BRAISED RED CABBAGE AND SMOKED BACON

Grated zest and juice of 2 oranges
12 fresh sage leaves, chopped
6 tablespoons virgin olive oil
½ cup red wine vinegar
6 bay leaves
1 tablespoon cracked black pepper
6 duck breasts, boned and skin pricked all over with
  a fork
Braised Red Cabbage (recipe follows)
12 bacon slices, preferably apple-cured, cooked until
  crisp
Fresh sage leaves (garnish)
Zest of ½ orange, cut into julienne (garnish)

Combine orange zest and juice, chopped sage, olive oil, vinegar, bay leaves, and pepper in a bowl. Add duck breasts and marinate, refrigerated, several hours or overnight, turning several times.

Prepare coals or preheat broiler.

Allow duck breasts to reach room temperature before slowly grilling them over medium-hot charcoal. Sear directly over coals for about 2 minutes per side, then place breasts over indirect heat, cover grill, and cook, turning once and basting occasionally with marinade, until skin is crisp but breast remains pink inside, about 10 minutes per side. (In absence of a charcoal grill, duck can be cooked under a preheated broiler.) When done, slice diagonally and arrange on top of hot Braised Red Cabbage and garnish with 2 bacon slices, fresh sage leaves, and orange zest.

Serves 6.

Grilled duck breast with braised red cabbage and smoked bacon.

BRAISED RED CABBAGE

¼ cup chopped bacon, preferably apple-cured
2 tablespoons butter
1 small head red cabbage, cored and thinly sliced
Juice of 1 lemon
5 tablespoons red wine vinegar
3 tablespoons homemade beef stock or canned low-
*   sodium broth*
1 tablespoon sugar or to taste
Salt
Freshly ground black pepper

In a sauté pan or skillet over medium-high heat, sauté bacon in butter until translucent; add cabbage and cook lightly, about 3 minutes. Add remaining ingredients, including salt and pepper to taste, reduce heat to medium-low, and cook until cabbage is slightly limp but still crisp, about 4 to 5 minutes.

Serves 6.

Strawberry shortcake.

STRAWBERRY SHORTCAKE

2 cups self-rising flour
½ cup sugar
¾ cup (1½ sticks) unsalted butter
2½ cups heavy cream
Additional cream for brushing
Sugar
2 pints fresh strawberries

Preheat oven to 450° F.

Combine flour and sugar in a mixing bowl. Cut butter into flour mixture until pieces are size of small peas. Fold in 1½ cups cream until dough starts to bind, then place on a well-floured counter and knead briefly just until it binds together, being careful not to over-knead. Roll out to 1 inch thick and cut into six 3 to 4-inch rounds. Place on a well-greased baking sheet, brush tops with cream, and sprinkle with sugar. Bake until golden brown, about 12 to 15 minutes.

Meanwhile, whip remaining cup of cream and sweeten to taste. Set aside.

Slice each shortcake in half. Place bottom half on each of 6 serving plates and cover with fresh strawberries and a dollop of whipped cream. Put top half over this and add another dollop of whipped cream and garnish with more strawberries.

Serves 6.

PERRY'S

*S*INCE THE LATE 1960S, Perry Butler's watering hole and eatery has been identified by many as the quintessential single's bar. This bastion of conviviality, immortalized in Armistead Maupin's *Tales of the City,* continues to pack them in for the daily cocktail hour. Food, sometimes relegated to second place in deference to the bar, runs the gamut from breakfast and brunch specialties, featured in the menu here, through definitive burgers and fries to grilled fish and chicken.

Movie and sports memorabilia cover the walls. Classic blue and white checked tablecloths add to the comfortable atmosphere that makes Perry's a second home to many.

Chef Nabil Massarweh began his career at the bottom of Perry's totem pole, gradually working his way up to his present position. His menu for a hearty brunch offers a choice between a classic presentation of onion soup crowned with melted cheese or a crisp salad generously smothered in bleu cheese. Like a visit to Perry's, the Apple Brown Betty is homey and comforting.

Chef Nabil Massarweh's
Menu for Eight

Sautéed Chicken Livers on Toast

Carmenet Sauvignon Blanc

□

Onion Soup Gratinée or Roquefort Salad

□

Eggs Blackstone

□

Apple Brown Betty

OPPOSITE, TOP: Perry's variation on a loaf of bread and a jug of wine. OPPOSITE, BOTTOM: Owner Perry Butler.
ABOVE: One of San Francisco's most popular bars since 1969.

Regular patrons enjoy the homey atmosphere.

SAUTÉED CHICKEN LIVERS ON TOAST

1 cup (2 sticks) butter
2 medium-sized yellow onions, chopped
2 pounds chicken livers, trimmed and large ones
  cut in half
1 teaspoon crumbled dried sage leaves
¼ cup diced prosciutto
Salt
Freshly ground black pepper
12 mushrooms, thinly sliced
¼ cup chopped fresh parsley
½ cup Marsala
2 tablespoons soft butter
8 pieces white toast, crusts removed
Additional chopped fresh parsley (garnish)

Melt butter in a large sauté pan or skillet,
add chopped onion, and sauté over medium-
high heat for 2 to 3 minutes. Add livers, sage,
prosciutto, and a sprinkle of salt and pepper.
Shake pan or stir frequently for 2 to 3 minutes,
then add sliced mushrooms. Continue to shake
pan frequently, turning chicken livers until
they are browned all over but still pink inside,
approximately 5 minutes. Add parsley and
Marsala and cook for 1 to 2 minutes over high
heat. Remove pan from heat and stir in soft
butter until it melts.

Serve hot over pieces of toast that have been
quartered diagonally. Garnish with additional
chopped parsley.

Serves 8 as appetizer.

Onion Soup Gratinée

8 large yellow onions, thinly sliced
1/4 cup butter
1 tablespoon olive oil
1 teaspoon salt
1 teaspoon sugar
1/4 cup flour
4 cups homemade chicken stock or canned low-sodium
   broth
4 cups homemade beef stock or canned low-sodium broth
1/2 cup dry sauterne
3 tablespoons brandy
Salt
Freshly ground black pepper
6 to 8 croutons of well-toasted French bread, cut to fit
   soup crocks
18 to 32 thick slices (about 1 pound) Gruyère,
   Emmentaler, or other easily melted cheese

Place onions in a covered saucepan with butter
and olive oil over low heat and cook, stirring
occasionally, until soft, about 30 minutes. Remove cover, add salt and sugar, and cook until
onions are golden brown, about 1 to 1½ hours,
stirring frequently to prevent burning. Stir in
flour and cook an additional 5 minutes.

In a separate saucepan over high heat, bring
chicken and beef stocks to a boil. Add cooked
onions and sauterne, return to a boil, then cover,
reduce heat, and simmer 45 minutes. Before
serving add brandy and salt and pepper to taste.

Preheat broiler.

Ladle soup into individual ovenproof crocks,
filling nearly to tops. Add a crouton to each bowl
and cover with 3 or 4 slices of cheese to cover
entire top of crock. Place crocks in a broiling
pan and position under broiler until cheese
melts, browns lightly, and forms a crust over
top of crock.

Serves 6 to 8.

Sautéed chicken livers served with toast.

Roquefort Salad

1 head each red, butter, and romaine lettuces
Perry's House Dressing (recipe follows)
1 pint cherry tomatoes, stemmed
1 cup (about 6 ounces) crumbled Roquefort cheese

Wash, dry, and chill lettuce leaves until serving
time.

In a large bowl, combine greens with Perry's
House Dressing to taste, tomatoes, and half of
cheese. Toss well. Serve on chilled plates and top
with remaining cheese.

Serves 8.

Perry's House Dressing

1 cup olive oil
1/3 cup red wine vinegar
1 1/2 teaspoons burgundy wine
1/4 teaspoon Tabasco sauce
1/4 teaspoon Worcestershire sauce
3/4 teaspoon dry mustard
3/4 teaspoon chopped fresh parsley
1/4 teaspoon dried basil
1/2 teaspoon celery seeds
1/2 teaspoon dried oregano
1/2 teaspoon dried thyme

Combine all ingredients in a mixing bowl,
blender, or jar and mix well.

Makes about 1½ cups.

EGGS BLACKSTONE

24 bacon slices
8 English muffins
2 tablespoons butter
8 ½-inch-thick tomato slices
16 eggs
Hollandaise Sauce (recipe follows)

Cook bacon until crisp; blot dry with paper towels and crumble into small pieces. Reserve.

Fork-split and toast muffins. Melt butter in a sauté pan or skillet and cook tomato slices on both sides. Meanwhile poach eggs in simmering water.

To serve, place a cooked tomato slice on top of each muffin half, then add a sprinkling of crumbled bacon and a poached egg. Cover generously with Hollandaise Sauce and garnish with an additional pinch of crumbled bacon.

Serves 8.

Eggs Blackstone features tomato slices.

Chef Nabil Massarweh.

HOLLANDAISE SAUCE

1 pound (4 sticks) butter
8 egg yolks
6 tablespoons freshly squeezed lemon juice
Cayenne pepper

Cut butter into 12 pieces approximately the same size. In top of a double boiler over water that is simmering but not boiling, place egg yolks, lemon juice, and 4 pieces butter. Stir rapidly with a wire whisk until butter melts. Add remaining pieces of butter one at a time, stirring until each melts before adding next piece. When all remaining butter has been added, stir in a dash of cayenne. Keep over warm water until ready to serve.

NOTE: The sauce will thicken the longer it sits over heat. If it gets too thick or starts to curdle, add a small amount of boiling water while stirring in order to obtain the right consistency.

Makes about 2½ cups.

APPLE BROWN BETTY

10 medium-sized apples
4 tablespoons ground cinnamon
¾ teaspoon ground nutmeg
¾ teaspoon salt
3 tablespoons sugar
1 tablespoon freshly squeezed lemon juice
1¼ cups clarified butter (see note)
1½ cups brown sugar
2½ cups all-purpose flour
1 cup heavy cream, whipped

Peel, core, and slice apples and place in bottom
of an 8 x 12-inch baking dish. Sprinkle with
1 tablespoon cinnamon, ¼ teaspoon nutmeg,
¼ teaspoon salt, sugar, lemon juice, and ¼ cup
clarified butter.

Preheat oven to 325° F.

In a bowl combine brown sugar, flour, remaining
1 cup clarified butter, ½ teaspoon salt, 3 tablespoons cinnamon, and ½ teaspoon nutmeg.
Sprinkle over top of apples and bake for approximately 1 hour and 15 minutes. Serve hot
with whipped cream. (Can be made ahead and
reheated.)

Serves 8.

NOTE: To clarify butter, melt about 1½ cups
(3 sticks) butter in a saucepan over low heat.
Remove from heat and let cool for a few minutes
while milk solids settle to bottom of pan. Skim
butterfat from top and strain clear clarified
butter into a container.

Perry's patio is a popular lunch spot.

PREGO

"**P**REGO'S supposed to look like it's been here forever, but at the same time look as fresh as though it just opened," explains General Manager Stanley Morris of this Italian-style grill, which actually opened its doors in 1981. The contemporary gray upholstery, white linen, Parmesan-colored walls, polished brass rails, and granite-topped bar stand up to such a test.

The extremely personable Morris was sidetracked from a career in urban planning by a University of Oregon–days job with the acclaimed Excelsior Café, the "Chez Panisse of the Northwest." He was quickly hooked on running a restaurant based on the finest and freshest ingredients available. When Prego opened, his friend Doug Biederbeck (now manager of the Fog City Diner) lured him down to the City. Soon he was running the restaurant, which he describes as a "sincere, neighborhood, Florentine-style *trattoria* that takes good care of the locals, people who appreciate good food and keep us on our toes."

Chef Robert Estenzo, originally from Berkeley, studied cooking in Florence and appreciates both California and Italian foods. He adapts the best of both worlds, although the stated goal of Prego's kitchen is to be as authentically Italian as possible. Prego, as Stanley Morris puts it, "stays away from nouvelle style and stays close to the land, going to great lengths to procure the very best ingredients from both California and Italy."

Chef Robert Estenzo's Menu for Six

Focaccia al Formaggio
Cinqueterre, Agricoltura di Riomaggiore, 1984

□

Insalata Mista

□

Conchiglie al Carciofo
La Battistina, Gavi, 1984

□

Galletto al Mattone
Monte Vertine, Le Pergole Torte, 1981

□

Meringata alla Cioccolata

OPPOSITE: Italian antipasti. ABOVE: Abundant food displays establish the Florentine atmosphere.

A friendly atmosphere invites dining alone.

FOCACCIA AL FORMAGGIO
(Flat Bread with Cheese)

Pizza Dough (recipe follows)
1 egg beaten with 1 tablespoon water
10 ounces Gorgonzola cheese
Fresh oregano leaves
Chopped fresh basil
Chopped fresh parsley
5 green onions, chopped
Extra-virgin olive oil

Preheat oven to 500° F.

Roll dough as thin as possible and put on a greased pizza pan. Brush with egg wash. Crumble cheese on top, then sprinkle with fresh herbs, green onions, and a little olive oil. Bake until cheese is melted and bubbly and crust is golden brown, about 5 minutes. Cut into small pieces and serve as an appetizer.

Serves 6.

PIZZA DOUGH

½ package active dry yeast
½ cup lukewarm water
2 cups all-purpose flour
1 tablespoon olive oil
½ teaspoon salt

Dissolve yeast in water. Add other ingredients and knead until elastic. Let rest a few minutes before rolling out. (No risings are required.)

INSALATA MISTA
(Salad of Radicchio, Watercress, Tomato, Leek, and Fresh Fennel)

3 bunches mâche (lamb's lettuce)
¾ pound radicchio
2 bunches watercress, stems removed
¾ cup thinly sliced leeks
¾ pound sweet fennel, thinly sliced crosswise
3 tomatoes, preferably vine-ripened, quartered
Extra-virgin olive oil
Red wine vinegar
Salt
Freshly ground pepper

Wash, dry, and chill lettuce and *radicchio* leaves.

Combine greens, leeks, fennel, and tomatoes in a salad bowl. Add olive oil, vinegar, salt and pepper to taste. Toss well and serve immediately.

Serves 6.

CONCHIGLIE AL CARCIOFO
(Tiny Pasta Shells with Artichokes, Pancetta, Cream, and Cheese)

¾ pound pancetta, diced
¾ cup (1½ sticks) butter
1 pound fresh artichoke hearts, well trimmed, cooked, and quartered

General manager Stanley Morris.

3 cups heavy cream
6 egg yolks
1 cup grated Parmesan cheese plus extra for passing
1½ pounds small pasta shells

In a sauté pan or skillet, sauté *pancetta* over medium-high heat until lightly browned and discard grease. Add butter and artichoke quarters and sauté briefly. In a bowl, mix together cream and egg yolks and add to *pancetta* mixture with ½ cup Parmesan. Reduce over low heat to sauce consistency.

Meanwhile, cook the pasta in 4 to 5 quarts boiling water until *al dente*, then drain and place in a warmed bowl. Pour sauce over pasta, then add remaining ½ cup Parmesan. Toss quickly and serve. Pass additional Parmesan at the table.

Serves 6.

GALLETTO AL MATTONE

(Grilled Lime-and Sage-marinated Whole Young Chicken)

6 20-ounce game hens or poussins (*baby chickens weighing under 1 pound*)
1½ cups extra-virgin olive oil
Juice of 18 limes
18 fresh sage leaves, chopped
6 garlic cloves, crushed
3 lemons, halved

With poultry shears, remove and discard spine of each bird, then open and flatten bird with hands.

Combine olive oil, lime juice, sage, and garlic and marinate birds, covered, in refrigerator for several hours or overnight, turning occasionally. Return to room temperature before grilling.

Prepare coals or preheat broiler.

Grill over charcoal or under a preheated broiler until skin is crisp and dark, about 20 to 30 minutes. Serve each bird with half a lemon.

Serves 6.

Cheese-topped flat bread with salad of mixed Italian greens.

MERINGATA ALLA CIOCCOLATA
(Meringue with Chocolate Cream)

2 meringues, about 8 inches across and 1 inch thick
  (use a basic recipe)
3 cups heavy cream
3 tablespoons plus 2 teaspoons cocoa
⅔ cup sugar
4 ounces fresh Italian Mascarpone *cheese or whipped*
  cream cheese
¾ teaspoon vanilla extract
⅓ cup white creme de menthe
6 ounces (6 squares) semisweet chocolate, chopped or
  shaved amaretti *cookies, crumbled (optional)*

Prepare meringues and set aside.

In a mixing bowl, combine cream, cocoa, sugar, *Mascarpone,* and vanilla; whip until stiff. Fold in crème de menthe. Place a meringue on a serving dish and spread about one-third of whipped mixture over it, then sprinkle one-third of chopped or shaved chocolate over whipped mixture. Put remaining meringue on top and cover top and sides with remaining whipped mixture. Sprinkle remaining chocolate and *amaretti* crumbs over top and sides.

Serves 6 to 8.

Chef Robert Estenzo in front of his pizza oven.

Grilled poussin with garden fresh vegetables.

Luscious sweets are the creation of pastry chef Cecile Getty.

RINGS

"*F*INE SEASONAL CUISINE," written under the name in the window, sums up the philosophy of brother-and-sister-team Dennis and Julie Ring. Dennis, a San Francisco painting contractor for twelve years, lured his sister Julie away from Chicago where she'd been a chef for six years, working her way up through pastry, soups, and salads to executive chef at two northern-Italian-style restaurants. To complete the family circle, Julie and Dennis's father moved to San Francisco to become the dinner host.

Fiery and friendly Julie calls her cooking "eclectic ethnic." It's heavy on Italian because of her Chicago background. A year in Mexico, a shared life with a Southern man, and varied travels all influence her dishes. No matter which nationality she's cooking, however, she tries to keep it authentic. "There's no *jícama* in my Italian pasta." Her French fries are from a variety of cultures. Thin crisp *pommes frites* are doused British style with vinegar, except that it's Asian rice vinegar, and liberally sprinkled with red chili flakes.

When Rings opened in 1985, lunch was mainly a neighborhood gathering of photographers, filmmakers, artists, and designers who work in the South of Market area. Dinner brought back some of the same, plus a lot of gay men who'd departed the declining South of Market leather bar scene but returned to reminisce. After a *San Francisco Focus* magazine feature, the reservation list nearly doubled, and includes nearby financial district people added to the lunch crowd and a cross-section of the City at dinner.

Dennis, who manages the business, chose the pink-highlighted-with-turquoise color scheme and directed the design, which includes a glass brick bar, the best place to sit and watch the cooking, chat with Julie, and feel the heat from the mesquite-fired grill.

Chef-owner Julie Ring's Menu for Four

King Salmon-stuffed Ravioli with Sorrel Cream

Saintsbury Garnet Pinot Noir, 1983

□

Grilled Ahi Tuna with Oregano Salsa Verde

□

Grilled Boneless Quail with Pecan Rice Stuffing in Roasted Pepper Cream

Mexican Corn Pudding

Dolan Chardonnay, 1983

□

Upside-down Pecan Apple Pie

Graham's Late Bottle Vintage, 1979

ABOVE: Ravioli stuffed with salmon and served with sorrel cream.

Ahi tuna and vegetables on mesquite grill.

KING SALMON-STUFFED RAVIOLI WITH SORREL CREAM

2 tablespoons butter
3 shallots, minced
1 garlic clove, chopped
1 cup (8 ounces) very fresh ricotta cheese
1 cup plus 5 tablespoons (about 10 ounces) grated
Asiago cheese
1 pound fresh king salmon, skinned and chopped
Ground white pepper
1½ cup unbleached all-purpose flour
1 teaspoon salt
3 eggs
1 tablespoon extra-virgin olive oil
1 cup fresh sorrel leaves
2 cups heavy cream
Fresh sorrel leaves, quickly fried in hot oil and
drained (garnish)

To make filling, melt butter in a sauté pan or
skillet over medium-high heat, add shallots and
garlic, and cook until soft, about 3 to 5 minutes.
Place in a blender or food processor with ricotta,
1 cup Asiago, salmon, and white pepper to
taste. Mix until thoroughly blended. Refrigerate
until cold.

To make pasta, combine flour, salt, and 2 eggs in
a mixing bowl. Mix slowly, adding olive oil; be
careful not to overwork dough. Following manu-
facturer's instructions, run dough through pasta
machine to knead, then form thin sheets. Size
and number of sheets will vary according to type
of pasta machine.

To make sauce, place sorrel and cream in a saucepan and reduce by one third. Blend in a blender
or food processor until smooth. Return to saucepan over low heat and whisk in remaining 5
tablespoons Asiago. Reserve.

To assemble, lay sheets of pasta on a floured work
surface. Brush dough with remaining egg,
beaten. Place large spoonfuls of filling about
every 4 inches. Brush a second sheet with egg
and place wet side down over sheet with filling
on it. Cut into 3- to 4-inch squares with a pastry
wheel. Press edges to seal tightly.

Cook ravioli in plenty of salted boiling water until pasta is *al dente,* about 4 minutes. Drain. Arrange on individual plates, allowing 2 per person. Cover with sauce and garnish with fried sorrel.

Serves 4.

GRILLED AHI TUNA WITH OREGANO SALSA VERDE

1 bunch fresh parsley, stems discarded
1 bunch fresh oregano, stems discarded
2 tablespoons puréed garlic
1 small can anchovy fillets
2 tablespoons capers, drained
¼ cup freshly squeezed lemon juice
¾ cup extra-virgin olive oil
4 8-ounce ahi *tuna steaks*

To make sauce, combine all ingredients except tuna in a blender or food processor and blend thoroughly. Set aside.

Prepare coals or preheat broiler.

Grill tuna over mesquite coals or under a broiler until rare or medium-rare, about 3 to 4 minutes per side; it should remain pink inside. Serve with reserved room-temperature sauce.

Serves 4.

Diners enjoy upside-down apple pecan pie served with strawberry sauce.

Grilled boneless quail with pecan rice stuffing in roasted pepper cream.

GRILLED BONELESS QUAIL WITH PECAN RICE STUFFING IN ROASTED PEPPER CREAM

4 quail
4 red sweet peppers
1 cup pine nuts
1 cup Pecan Rice (available at quality food stores)
2 cups water
2 tablespoons butter
2 shallots, diced
2 tablespoons puréed garlic
1 cup chopped fresh basil
Salt
Freshly ground white pepper
2 cups heavy cream
Pinch cayenne pepper
Olive oil
Fresh basil leaves (garnish)

Place quail breast side down and cut down middle of back. Using a small sharp knife, begin at neck and cut flesh down and away from bones. Remove skeleton including breastbone; leave thigh and leg intact. Remove and discard wings if desired. Reserve.

Roast peppers over charcoal or gas flame or place under a broiler, turning several times, until skin is charred all over. Place in a loosely closed paper bag to cool for about 10 minutes. Rub away charred skin. Cut peppers in half, seed, devein, and slice. Reserve.

Place pine nuts in a small heavy frying pan over medium heat. Stir until they begin to turn golden, about 5 minutes. Remove from heat and pour onto a plate to cool.

Cook Pecan Rice in water according to package directions. In a small pan over medium-high heat, melt butter and sauté shallots, garlic, basil, and toasted pine nuts until shallots and garlic are soft, about 3 to 5 minutes. Combine with cooked rice, add salt and pepper to taste, and stuff into quail cavities. Tie quail closed with cotton string to hold stuffing in place.

Combine roasted peppers, cream, and cayenne in a saucepan and cook until reduced by half, then transfer to a blender or food processor and purée until smooth. Reserve.

Prepare coals or preheat broiler.

Brush stuffed quail with olive oil and grill over a low mesquite fire or under a broiler for 15 minutes, turning to brown evenly. Coat each serving plate with sauce and arrange one quail on top. Garnish with basil leaves.

Serves 4.

MEXICAN CORN PUDDING

(Recipe by Diego Michel)

About 6 ears fresh corn, enough to make 2½ cups
    corn kernels
2 tablespoons soft unsalted butter
2 eggs, separated
½ teaspoon baking powder
Salt
2 teaspoons sugar
Grated Asiago cheese

Chef Julie Ring.

Cut corn from cob, scraping with back of knife to collect juices. Place in a blender or food processor and purée until smooth. Reserve.

Preheat oven to 400° F.

Mix butter well with egg yolks and combine with puréed corn. Add baking powder and salt to taste, mix well, and set aside.

Beat egg whites, adding sugar gradually, until stiff peaks form. Gently fold into corn mixture. Pour into buttered and floured 8-inch-square pan. Sprinkle with cheese and bake until golden brown and center feels set when touched, about 30 minutes.

Serves 4.

UPSIDE-DOWN PECAN APPLE PIE

(Patti Johnson, pastry chef)

3 cups plus 1½ tablespoons all-purpose flour
1½ cups (3 sticks) unsalted butter
¼ teaspoon salt
⅓ cup plus ½ teaspoon sugar
⅓ cup cold water
¾ cup brown sugar
1⅓ cups chopped pecans
4 green apples, peeled, cored, and cut into ¼-inch-
    thick slices
1 teaspoon ground cinnamon
Grated zest of 1 lemon
1 tablespoon freshly squeezed lemon juice

To make dough, combine 3 cups flour, 1 cup butter, salt, and ½ teaspoon sugar in food processor and run until texture of cornmeal. While processing, add water and run 10 seconds. Remove from machine and form into a ball. (Dough can be made by hand by blending ingredients with two knives or a pastry blender.) Divide into one-third and two-thirds pieces. Wrap in plastic and refrigerate.

Flowers in glass block.

To make topping, combine remaining ½ cup butter, brown sugar, and pecans in a mixing bowl and mix thoroughly. Pour into a 9-inch deep-dish round pan, spreading evenly on bottom of pan. Set aside.

To make filling, combine apples, cinnamon, remaining ⅓ cup sugar and 1½ tablespoons flour with lemon zest and juice in a large bowl. Mix together, coating all apples.

Preheat oven to 350° F.

On a floured board roll larger piece of dough into an 11-inch circle. Place in pan on top of pecan mixture. Pour in apples. Roll small piece of dough into 9½-inch circle. Brush edge of bottom piece of dough with water, place second piece of dough on top of apples, and seal closed by bringing bottom edge over top edge and crimping with fingers to form a pattern. Make steam cuts on top of pie and bake on a baking sheet until golden brown, about 50 minutes. Cool 1 minute, then invert onto a plate and remove pan.

Serves 6.

ROSALIE'S

*L*OOKING MORE LIKE it belongs in Los Angeles than in San Francisco, Rosalie's was obviously inspired by the black and white Hollywood movie musicals of the 1930's. The silver screen is echoed in metal palm fronds sprouting from mirrored square trunks, and uncovered galvanized tin tabletops set against a background of grays. Bold splashes of Technicolor hues do manage to sneak in along the back wall. Unlike most San Francisco restaurants, there's not a flower or plant in sight, except for one big changing display in the center of an entry tent with curtains of white molded plaster.

The silvery fantasy decor was designed by owner Bill Belloli, a former model, designer, and retailer. His partner Bill Miller comes from a financial background. The team opened Rosalie's in 1985 because they were tired of working for other people.

Warmth is added to the restaurant by an attractive and friendly staff and by the seasonal food turned out by Chef James Geof Felsenthal. Like the chefs at Fog City Diner, Gaylord, and Rings, he is another Chicago defector to the San Francisco restaurant scene. After graduating from the California Culinary Academy, the young chef moved from Campton Place to Rosalie's as a line cook, then a sous-chef, before being quickly promoted when the original chef departed shortly after the restaurant opened.

Felsenthal uses his classical training to create innovative dishes, working twelve-to-fifteen-hour days not only cooking but researching new ingredients. Modestly, he describes Rosalie's kitchen as the result of teamwork instead of the efforts of a star chef, although he sees himself as being on stage each night, auditioning for a new audience and finding instant gratification from cooking.

Chef James Geof Felsenthal's Menu for Six

Pear Salad

Sauvignon Blanc

□

Baked Oysters with Garlic and Almond Butter

Gewürztraminer

□

Veal Chop Stuffed with Spinach, Pine Nuts, and Chanterelle Mushrooms

Sautéed Snow Peas

Fresh Fettuccine

Chardonnay

□

Warm Banana Split

Champagne or Late Harvest Dessert Wine

OPPOSITE: Trompe l'oeil tented entrance. ABOVE: Garlic and almond butter flavor baked oysters.

PEAR SALAD

6 ounces blue cheese, preferably Maytag, at room
    temperature
3 ounces cream cheese, at room temperature
¹⁄₃ cup minced black walnuts
5 ripe Bosc or d'Anjou pears
¹⁄₂ cup pear vinegar
1 cup olive oil
¹⁄₂ teaspoon salt
¹⁄₂ teaspoon freshly ground pepper
1 bunch chives, snipped
2 medium-sized heads radicchio, *cut into*
    chiffonnade
2 medium-sized heads Belgium endive, spears separated
1 bunch watercress, large stems removed
¹⁄₃ cup black walnut pieces

Blend cheeses and minced walnuts together and
reserve.

Core whole pears with an apple corer, removing
seeds and leaving a cavity about the diameter of
a quarter. Fill pears with reserved cheese mixture, making sure cavities are well stuffed. Chill
for 1 hour.

To make vinaigrette, whisk vinegar and oil
together in a small bowl until emulsified, then
add salt, pepper, and chives.

To assemble, toss *radicchio* with just enough
vinaigrette to lightly coat; place on lower half of
each of 6 individual plates. With a sharp knife,
cut pears into ¼-inch-thick circles, being careful
not to press too hard. Arrange 5 pear slices over
radicchio on each plate. Lightly coat endive with
vinaigrette and arrange 5 spears on each plate in
a fan shape above pear slices. Garnish with
watercress between pear slices and endive and a
cluster of black walnuts at bottom of each plate.

Serves 6.

Soft sculpture dancers add to the fantasy.

Galvanized tin bar with entry tent in background.

BAKED OYSTERS WITH GARLIC AND ALMOND BUTTER

1½ cups (3 sticks) soft unsalted butter
6 thin prosciutto slices
3 shallots
6 garlic cloves
¾ cup whole almonds, toasted and chopped (see note)
½ bunch parsley, coarsely chopped
1 bunch chives, coarsely chopped
Juice of 1 lemon
2 tablespoons dry white wine
1½ teaspoons salt
2 teaspoons freshly ground black pepper
36 oysters
Rock salt
French bread for dipping

To make compound butter, place butter, pro-sciutto, shallots, garlic, ½ cup toasted almonds, parsley, chives, lemon juice, wine, salt, and pepper in a blender or food processor. Blend carefully to achieve a smooth butter that still shows off ingredients. Reserve.

Preheat oven to 375° F.

Shuck oysters, retaining bottom shells and juice in shells if possible. Place oysters-on-the-half-shell in a bed of rock salt on a baking sheet, jelly roll pan, or shallow ovenproof serving dishes. Place a small amount of reserved compound butter on each oyster. Heat in oven until butter has melted and oysters have firmed up a bit. Garnish with remaining toasted almonds. Serve with warm French bread to dip into shells.

Serves 6.

NOTE: To toast almonds, place them in a small heavy ovenproof skillet in a preheated 350° F oven, stirring frequently, until lightly browned, about 10 to 15 minutes. Pour onto a plate to cool, then chop.

VEAL CHOP STUFFED WITH SPINACH, PINE NUTS, AND CHANTERELLE MUSHROOMS

3 tablespoons olive oil
3 garlic cloves, minced
3 shallots, minced
1 pound 5 ounces fresh chanterelle mushrooms, sliced
¾ cup dry white wine
3 bunches fresh spinach, washed well, dried, and
*   coarsely chopped*
1 small bunch fresh sage leaves
1 tablespoon whole-grain mustard
⅔ cup pine nuts, lightly toasted and chopped (see note)
1 teaspoon salt
1½ teaspoons freshly ground black pepper
6 12- to 14-ounce veal chops, about 2 inches thick
1 tablespoon crumbled dried sage leaves
1 cup homemade chicken stock or canned low-
*   sodium broth*
Salt
Freshly ground black pepper
4 tablespoons unsalted butter

Heat 2 tablespoons olive oil in a sauté pan or
skillet over medium-high heat, add garlic and
2 chopped shallots, and sauté 1 minute. Add
1 pound 2 ounces mushrooms and cook until
tender, about 5 minutes. Add ¼ cup wine and
cook until almost dry, about 10 minutes. Remove
from heat and add spinach, fresh sage, mustard,
pine nuts, salt, and pepper. Toss until spinach
is wilted and well mixed. Cool.

Preheat oven to 425° F.

With a sharp knife, cut a slit in middle of each
veal chop to form a pocket and stuff with spinach
mixture.

Intimate banquets in an ultramodern setting at Rosalie's.

Heat remaining 1 tablespoon olive oil in an ovenproof sauté pan or skillet over high heat. Brown chops on both sides and transfer to oven for 8 to 10 minutes. Remove chops and deglaze pan with remaining ½ cup wine, scraping bottom of pan. Add remaining shallot and 3 ounces mushrooms along with dried sage and cook until reduced by half; add chicken stock and salt and pepper to taste and reduce again by half. Add butter and heat until melted. Pour over veal chops. Serve with sautéed fresh snow peas and *fettuccine* cooked *al dente*.

Serves 6.

NOTE: To toast pine nuts, place them in a small heavy skillet over medium heat. Stir until they begin to turn golden. Remove from heat and pour onto a plate to cool.

Chef James Geof Felsenthal.

WARM BANANA SPLIT

6 ripe but firm bananas
Chocolate and vanilla ice cream
Chocolate Sauce (recipe follows)
Caramel Sauce (recipe follows)
Sweetened whipped cream (garnish)
Fresh berries or sliced fruit such as mango, papaya, or kiwi (garnish)

Preheat oven to 400° F.

Place unpeeled bananas in oven until black, about 6 to 8 minutes. Cut in half lengthwise. Remove peel and place bananas on individual plates. Put one scoop of vanilla ice cream in curve of one banana half and a scoop of chocolate ice cream in curve of the other half. Cover vanilla ice cream with Chocolate Sauce, and chocolate ice cream with Caramel Sauce. Garnish with whipped cream and fresh fruit. Serve warm.

Serves 6.

CHOCOLATE SAUCE

1 pound semisweet chocolate, chopped
½ cup chopped pecans
½ cup chopped macadamia nuts
½ cup chopped walnuts

Melt chocolate in top of a double boiler over simmering water. When melted, add nuts. Serve warm.

Makes about 2 cups.

Warm banana split.

CARAMEL SAUCE

1 cup sugar
1½ cups water
1½ cups heavy cream, heated
4 tablespoons soft unsalted butter

Combine sugar and water in a small saucepan and cook over moderate heat until dark brown, about 8 to 10 minutes. Remove from heat and slowly add heated cream. Stir in butter until melted. Serve warm.

Makes about 2½ cups.

SAM'S GRILL

*L*ANDMARK SAM'S is the successor to an 1867 oyster saloon, M. B. Moraghan and Sons, in the old California Market. By the mid-1890s, Moraghan's was a huge combination oyster bar, seafood restaurant, and fresh-fish emporium. The restaurant was purchased in 1922 by Yugoslavian immigrant Sam Zenovich, who changed the name to Samuel Zenovich Restaurant, popularly dubbed Sam's. When Zenovich died in 1937, the business was purchased by Frank Seput, who modified the name to Sam's Grill and Sea Food Restaurant and continued to operate in the original location until 1945 when Sam's was moved to the present Bush Street location.

Genial owner-host Gary Seput is the third generation of his family to operate Sam's, which has stayed busy since the day it opened. Today, you wait your turn at the small bar at the front of the restaurant for one of the private curtained cubicles, or for a crisp white linen-laid table in the dark wood-paneled dining room. Hooks along the walls invite the financial district crowd to hang their suit jackets while they enjoy lunch.

For the past thirty years Sam's has cooked fish and meats over mesquite, a method which the menu identifies as "charcoal-broiled" instead of the more current "grilled." Sam's is best known for charcoal-broiled West Coast fish, especially petrale, sand dabs, and salmon, although the very popular, delicate, boned rex sole is always pan-cooked, never grilled. There's also an array of shellfish dishes including Hangtown Fry, an Old San Francisco original combination of eggs, bacon, and oysters.

Owner Gary Seput's Menu for Eight

Coney Island Clam Chowder

Sourdough Bread

□

Sam's Special Seafood Salad

□

Deviled Crab à la Sam

Fresh Asparagus

Steamed Carrots

Burgess or Edna Valley Chardonnay

□

Chocolate Kahlúa Cake with Strawberry Sauce

OPPOSITE: A steady stream of patrons have passed through the doors since 1945. ABOVE: Curtained wooden cubicles provide privacy and atmosphere.

Individual compartments are reminiscent of early San Francisco restaurants.

CONEY ISLAND CLAM CHOWDER

24 fresh medium-sized clams, or ½ pound frozen clams
4 cups water
1 large onion, minced
½ celery stalk, diced
1 green sweet pepper, diced
¼ cup vegetable oil
2 tablespoons flour
1½ cups stewed tomatoes
2 medium-sized potatoes, peeled and diced
Salt

In a large stockpot over high heat, add just enough water to cover clams and boil just until shells open. Drain, reserving cooking liquid. Shuck clams and reserve.

In a deep pot over medium-high heat, sauté onion, celery, and pepper in oil until vegetables are tender, about 10 minutes. Add flour and stir to blend. Bring reserved clam cooking liquid to a boil and add to vegetables, stir until smooth, and bring to a soft boil. Add tomatoes with their liquid and bring to a boil again. Add potatoes and simmer until potatoes are tender, about 10 to 15 minutes. Add clams and salt to taste; bring to a boil. Serve hot with sourdough French bread.

Serves 8 as first course; 4 as main course.

SAM'S SPECIAL SEAFOOD SALAD

8 celery hearts (inner stalks), without leaves, steamed
*   and chilled*
2 avocados, peeled and thinly sliced
2 cups bay shrimp, cooked and chilled
2 cups cooked fresh crab meat, picked over
24 medium-sized prawns, cooked, peeled, deveined,
*   and chilled*
8 anchovy fillets
2 medium-sized ripe tomatoes, sliced and cut into
*   half-circles*
Sam's House Dressing (recipe follows)
Chopped fresh parsley (garnish)

Arrange celery on 8 individual salad plates. Top with avocados and shellfish. Garnish with anchovies and tomatoes, drizzle with Sam's House Dressing to taste, and sprinkle with parsley.

Serves 8.

SAM'S HOUSE DRESSING

⅓ teaspoon salt
⅛ teaspoon freshly ground black pepper
⅛ teaspoon dry mustard
1 cup vegetable oil
¼ cup red wine vinegar

Combine salt, pepper, and mustard in a bowl. Blend well with a little oil. Add remaining oil and vinegar slowly while constantly blending.

Makes about 1¼ cups.

DEVILED CRAB À LA SAM

1½ cups vegetable oil
6 celery stalks, minced
2 medium-sized onions, minced
1 large green sweet pepper, minced
2 cups all-purpose flour
Dash of ground white pepper
Dash of ground nutmeg
3 tablespoons dry mustard
1½ quarts milk, scalded
2 pounds fresh cooked crab meat, picked over, or canned
*   crab meat, rinsed and drained*
½ cup freshly grated Parmesan cheese
Paprika
¼ cup melted butter

Heat oil in a saucepan over medium heat, add celery, onions, and green pepper, and cook slowly until tender, about 10 minutes. Add flour, white pepper, nutmeg, and dry mustard until well blended. Slowly add warm milk, stirring constantly with a wire whisk or wooden spoon until smooth. Add crab meat, stir well, and cook until mixture begins to boil; remove from heat.

Owner Gary Seput and chef Peter Lu.

Preheat oven to 400° F.

Pour crab with sauce into an ovenproof casserole or 8 individual serving dishes, sprinkle generously with Parmesan cheese, dust with paprika, and drizzle with melted butter. Bake in oven until golden brown, about 5 minutes. Serve immediately.

Serves 8.

CHOCOLATE KAHLÚA CAKE WITH STRAWBERRY SAUCE

½ cup (1 stick) unsalted butter
4 ounces (4 squares) semisweet chocolate
½ cup Kahlúa liqueur
3 eggs, separated
1 cup sugar
¾ cup sifted all-purpose flour
Pinch of salt
Strawberry Sauce (recipe follows)
Sweetened whipped cream (garnish)

Preheat oven to 350° F.

Melt butter and chocolate with Kahlúa in top of a double boiler set over simmering water. Using a wire whisk or electric mixer, beat egg yolks and sugar in a mixing bowl until mixture is pale yellow, then add melted chocolate mixture. Stir in flour to blend well. Beat egg whites to soft-peak stage and fold into batter. Pour into a round 8 x 1½-inch round cake pan and bake until a tester comes out clean, about 30 minutes. Let cool completely before serving plain or with Strawberry Sauce and a dollop of whipped cream.

Serves 8.

STRAWBERRY SAUCE

2 cups fresh ripe strawberries, stemmed
Sugar

Place strawberries in a blender or food processor and coarsely purée. Add sugar to taste and serve immediately or chilled.

Makes about 1 cup.

Sam's special seafood salad.

SQUARE ONE

YOU DON'T EXPECT to find a *magna cum laude Phi Beta Kappa* graduate of Smith College with a MFA from Yale University School of Art and Architecture up to her elbows in *gravlax*. But Joyce Goldstein, chef-owner of Square One, like so many other new American chefs, finds food her best field of expression, more exciting than exhibiting her paintings at the San Francisco Museum of Art.

Goldstein's food experiences include founding the award-winning California Street Cooking School, featured in national magazines including *Time* and *Newsweek*. In the early 1970s, she was a food reporter for KQED and a food writer for *Rolling Stone*. Author of *Feedback*, a book about cooking as communication, she is presently writing a kitchen column for *Bon Appetit* magazine. She has taught kitchen design in the Department of Architecture at the University of California, Berkeley, and was the planning consultant for I. Magnin's Edibles department.

After a stint as head chef, manager, and recipe planner for Chez Panisse Café, Goldstein says that opening her own restaurant in 1984 was the next logical step in her development. With such credentials it's easy to see why Joyce Goldstein was named to Who's Cooking in America by *The Cook's Magazine* in 1985.

Goldstein loves hard work, cooking almost every day as well as keeping up with the writing projects and doing all the paperwork herself. She admits to getting really grumpy on days she doesn't cook.

Her philosophy of food? "Number one: tasty. Not mysterious. Sensual and satisfying. Do it well and distinctively." Specialties are mostly classical dishes "because they are remembered." She enjoys an international range of ingredients, but stays within the genre of whatever she's cooking, avoiding mixing ethnic backgrounds.

Goldstein is justly proud of her partner-son Evan, whose wine list for Square One was named Best in America by *Wine Spectator* magazine.

Chef-owner Joyce Goldstein's Menu for Six

Toasted Almonds

Dry Amontillado Sherry

☐

Tomato Soup

☐

Paella

Sangría or Edna Valley Pinot Noir, 1982

☐

Salad of Belgian Endive, Watercress, Walnuts, and Pears
with Gorgonzola Cheese and Walnut Vinaigrette

☐

Tarta de Sevilla

OPPOSITE: Chef-owner Joyce Goldstein. ABOVE: Paella with lobster, clams, prawns, chorizo, artichokes, and saffron-infused rice.

The bar boasts one of the best wine lists in America.

TOMATO SOUP

2 large yellow onions, sliced
½ cup (1 stick) butter
12 large beefsteak or other flavorful tomatoes, quartered
Salt
Freshly ground black pepper

GARNISH: *(choose one)*
   fresh basil, cut into thin strips
   heavy cream with chopped fresh mint
   crème fraîche and chopped fresh basil or mint
   orange zest-flavored cream
   croutons with Parmesan
   croutons with Chèvre

Sauté onions in butter in a saucepan over medium-high heat until soft, about 8 to 10 minutes. Add tomatoes, stirring occasionally to prevent scorching, and cook until tomatoes are completely broken down and have given off a great deal of liquid, about 20 minutes. Pureé in a blender or food processor. Pass through a food mill to remove seeds and excessive peel.

Season to taste with salt and pepper. Reheat to serve. Garnish with any one of suggested items.

Serves 6.

VARIATION: Add a walnut-sized piece of ginger root, peeled and grated or minced, to onions while sautéing.

PAELLA

3 tablespoons dried oregano
3 tablespoons minced garlic
3 teaspoons salt
2 tablespoons coarsely ground black pepper
5 tablespoons red wine vinegar
6 to 8 tablespoons olive oil, plus about 1 cup for sautéing
12 chicken thighs, trimmed of excess fat
2 large yellow onions, chopped
2 tablespoons minced garlic
2 green sweet peppers, diced
2 cups diced flavorful ripe tomatoes or drained canned plum tomatoes
4 to 6 cups rich homemade chicken stock or canned low-sodium broth
4 cups long-grain rice, preferably basmati
5 quarts water, salted to taste
½ cup (1 stick) butter, melted
2 teaspoons saffron steeped in ¼ cup white wine or vermouth
6 large artichokes, all leaves and chokes removed, hearts pared and cut into sixths
Juice of 1 lemon
Salt
Freshly ground black pepper
1 pound chorizo, baked and cut into chunks
36 clams, steamed open, juices reserved

3 eastern lobsters, steamed for 5 to 6 minutes, then cut into chunks
1 pound prawns, cleaned and poached in stock for 1 minute, then peeled and deveined (optional)
½ cup fresh peas, blanched (optional)
2 red sweet peppers, roasted, peeled, and cut into strips

The day before you plan to serve, combine oregano, garlic, salt, black pepper, vinegar, and 6 to 8 tablespoons olive oil in a small bowl. Rub into chicken thighs and marinate overnight in refrigerator.

The next day, sauté chicken thighs in ½ cup olive oil in a sauté pan or skillet over medium-high heat until browned, about 10 minutes. Reserve.

In a separate pan over medium-high heat, sauté onions, garlic, and green peppers in ¼ cup olive oil until softened, about 10 minutes. Add tomatoes, chicken stock, and reserved chicken pieces. Bring to a boil, reduce heat to medium-low, and simmer until chicken is tender, about 20 to 25 minutes. Adjust seasonings to taste.

Preheat oven to 350° F.

Co-owner Evan Goldstein.

In a large stockpot, cook rice in boiling salted water for about 10 minutes. Drain, rinse with warm water, drain again, and place in a baking dish. Combine butter with saffron mixture, pour over rice, cover, and bake for 25 minutes.

Sauté artichoke hearts in remaining ¼ cup olive oil with lemon juice until tender but not mushy. Season to taste with salt and pepper. Reserve.

To serve, combine chicken mixture and juices, rice, artichokes, chorizo, clams and their juices, lobster, prawns, and peas and heat through. Garnish with pepper strips.

Serves 6 to 8.

SANGRÍA

2 oranges, thinly sliced
2 lemons, thinly sliced
2 limes, thinly sliced
1 bottle rioja wine
¼ cup brandy
1 large bottle club soda

In a large bowl or pitcher, combine orange, lemon, and lime slices with wine and brandy and macerate for a few hours. Add club soda and ice cubes just before serving.

Makes about 2 quarts.

SALAD OF BELGIAN ENDIVE, WATERCRESS, WALNUTS, AND PEARS WITH GORGONZOLA CHEESE AND WALNUT VINAIGRETTE

½ cup olive oil
¼ cup walnut oil
3 tablespoons balsamic vinegar
1 to 2 tablespoons sherry vinegar
Salt
Freshly ground black pepper

Salad of Belgian endive, watercress, walnuts, and pears with Gorgonzola cheese and walnut vinaigrette.

½ cup broken walnuts
2 ripe and buttery Comice pears or crisp Pippin or Granny Smith apples
4 heads Belgian endive, leaves separated
2 large bunches watercress, stemmed
12 ounces Gorgonzola, crumbled into walnut-sized pieces

Preheat oven to 350° F.

To make vinaigrette, combine olive and walnut oils, vinegars, and salt and pepper to taste in a small bowl; reserve.

Place walnuts in a small heavy ovenproof skillet in oven, stirring frequently, until lightly toasted, about 10 to 15 minutes. Pour onto a plate to cool.

Just before serving, slice unpeeled pears or apples. Toss endive and watercress with some reserved vinaigrette to taste and arrange on 6 individual plates. On each plate place 6 slices of pear or apple, 4 pieces of Gorgonzola, and evenly distribute walnut pieces over greens. Drizzle lightly with additional vinaigrette.

Serves 6.

TARTA DE SEVILLA

(Craig Sutter, pastry chef)

1 cup chopped almonds
3 tablespoons cornstarch
¼ cup milk
6 whole eggs, beaten
9 egg yolks, beaten
1 cup sugar
Grated zest of 6 lemons
Juice of 7 lemons
½ cup (1 stick) unsalted butter
¾ cup (1½ sticks) salted butter
½ teaspoon almond extract
1 tablespoon Amaretto
Pâté Brisée (recipe follows)
1 egg, beaten and combined with an equal portion of heavy cream
Sugar for sprinkling
Creme Chantilly (recipe follows)

Preheat oven to 350° F.

Place almonds in a small heavy ovenproof skillet in oven, stirring frequently, until lightly toasted, about 10 to 15 minutes. Pour onto plate and rub with fingers to remove skin.

Dissolve cornstarch in milk and combine in a heavy saucepan with eggs and yolks, sugar, lemon zest and juice, and butters. Cook over medium heat, stirring constantly, until custard is thick and coats the back of a spoon. Pour into a bowl or container, stirring in toasted almonds, extract, and Amaretto; cool.

Roll 2 pieces Pâté Brisée dough into circles about 1 inch larger than lip of a 9-inch pie pan, using enough flour on board to keep dough from sticking to board. Brush off excess flour from dough. Fit one circle into pie pan. Lay top crust on a baking sheet to rest in refrigerator.

To assemble, fill bottom crust to top with lemon filling. Brush edge of bottom crust with water, cover pie with refrigerated top crust, press to seal crusts together, and trim dough 1 inch larger than lip of pan. Fold excess dough under bottom crust so edge of dough meets edge of pan; press and shape edges of crusts together. Using fingers, pinch edge of crust to form a bold fluted pattern.

With a sharp knife, make a design in top crust, being sure to pierce through dough occasionally to allow steam to escape. Brush top crust with egg wash to glaze. Sprinkle with sugar and bake in preheated oven until crust is golden brown, about 1 to 1½ hours. Let cool completely before serving. Serve with Crème Chantilly.

Serves 8.

Pastry chef Craig Sutter.

PÂTÉ BRISÉE

1½ cups all-purpose flour
¼ teaspoon sugar
¾ cup (1½ sticks) salted butter, frozen
2 tablespoons shortening
2 tablespoons ice water
2 teaspoons freshly squeezed lemon juice

In a bowl, combine flour and sugar. Cut butter and shortening into small pieces, and work them into dry ingredients by rubbing butter and shortening with flour between your fingers until there are only dime-sized lumps in flour, or use a food processor or mixer. Combine ice water and lemon juice and gradually pour mixture into flour, mixing just enough to bring dough together. Divide dough into 2 equal parts and let rest a few minutes before wrapping in damp towels or plastic. Refrigerate 1 hour before rolling. Dough should have a marbled look when finished. When rolled out, this marbled effect creates the layers that cause the desired flakiness.

Makes 1 deep double-crust for a 9-inch pie.

NOTE: Both butter and shortening are needed to make successful pie crusts: butter for flavor and browning, shortening for flakiness. The addition of moisture washes starch and activates gluten in flour. When dough is overworked, gluten becomes tough and elastic; therefore this process should be stopped before it goes too far. Underworking dough so as to leave some moisture coating flour creates a better texture. Let dough sit out for a few minutes before wrapping, as flour will continue to absorb liquid. Wrap in damp cloths or plastic and refrigerate for at least 30 minutes to allow dough to rest before rolling.

CRÈME CHANTILLY

1 cup heavy cream
1 to 3 tablespoons sifted powdered sugar
½ teaspoon vanilla extract

Using a chilled wire whisk or beaters in a chilled copper or stainless steel bowl, whip cream just until it forms soft peaks and retains its glossiness; avoid overbeating. Fold in powdered sugar and vanilla.

Makes about 2 cups.

WASHINGTON SQUARE BAR & GRILL

WITHOUT DOUBT, The Washbag is San Francisco's most popular watering hole, a special haunt of media stars, writers, artists, and politicians. Even if you're not literary or famous, Ed and Mary Etta Moose make you feel at home in the totally unpretentious atmosphere that remains unchanged since they opened their doors in 1973. The secret of their success may be that the Mooses want everyone to have a good time whether at the bar or in the dining room.

While Ed is most likely found telling stories around the bar or managing the staff, the kitchen is Mary Etta's territory. She directs her young cooks in the North Beach style of Italian cooking, an endeavor with which she should feel comfortable. After all, she wrote the book on the subject (*The Flavor of North Beach,* available at the restaurant).

The Washington Square Bar & Grill may have the most loyal patronage of any restaurant in San Francisco. For many well-to-do North Beach bohemians, it is a club or a second home, complete with a slow-pitch softball team whose antics in international competition were recorded by *Sports Illustrated.*

First-timers at Washington Square Bar & Grill may be surprised by the small space and simple surroundings of such a notorious place. During off hours, the deep-wine walls give a somber feeling, but once the place is packed with people, as it is daily, it comes alive with color and excitement. It's a great place for people watching, revelry, and, in spite of one restaurant critic's opinion, a good place for food that captures the authentic flavor of North Beach.

Owner Mary Etta Moose's Menu for Six

WSB&G's Shaken Bloody Mary

□

*California Field Salad with Sweet Peppers
and Fennel in Basil Vinaigrette*

□

Sea Bass Ravioli in Sage Butter
Navarro Chardonnay, 1983

□

*Veal Chop en Papillote with Leeks
and Chanterelles*
Felton-Empire Pinot Noir, 1982

□

Coeur à la Crème with Berry Purée

□

C.B.A. per WSB&G

OPPOSITE: Owners (left to right) Mark Schachern, Ed and Mary Etta Moose, and chef Richard Oku. ABOVE: Coeur à la Creme with puree of strawberries.

The Washbag is probably the city's most popular watering hole.

WSB&G's Shaken Bloody Mary

Cracked ice or small ice cubes
1 cup plus 2 tablespoons vodka
1½ cups tomato juice, preferably Sacramento brand
¾ cup canned beef bouillon
¼ cup plus 2 tablespoons freshly squeezed lemon juice
6 dashes each Worcestershire and Tabasco sauces
Celery salt
Freshly ground pepper
6 lime wedges

Put ice into a glass-bottomed shaker. Pour in vodka, tomato juice, bouillon, lemon juice, and sauces, adding celery salt and pepper to taste. Shake and strain into six 6-ounce stemmed glasses. Squeeze lime into each glass as wedge is added to glass.

Serves 6.

California Field Salad with Sweet Peppers and Fennel in Basil Vinaigrette

Smallest possible head each butter lettuce, romaine,
*   Belgian endive, radicchio or chicoria Treviso,*
*   watercress or arugula, and red leaf lettuce*
1 bulb sweet fennel
1 medium-sized red sweet pepper
1 medium-size golden sweet pepper
Basil Vinaigrette (recipe follows)
Kosher salt
Freshly ground black pepper
Fresh basil leaves, cut into thin strips (garnish)

Separate leaves of lettuces and use only smallest inner leaves or hearts. (Set aside large outer leaves for another purpose.) Wash and dry leaves. Leave 2½-inch leaves whole; break longer leaves in half. Cut watercress into 2½- to 3-inch sprigs.

Tear *radicchio* leaves into manageable pieces. Store the dried greens in a plastic bag or airtight container until ready to serve.

Cut off and discard green tops of fennel. Cut bulb crosswise into enough paper-thin slices to sprinkle across tops of salads.

Seed and devein peppers and cut into half-inch dice. (They do not need to be roasted or peeled.)

To serve, toss greens, fennel, and sweet peppers with Basil Vinaigrette. Sprinkle with salt and pepper to taste. Toss again. Garnish with basil.

NOTE: If *radicchio* or *Treviso* is not available, use finely shredded red cabbage for color. If you can get *mâche* (lamb's lettuce) and/or limestone lettuce, substitute for butterhead and/or romaine.

Serves 6.

BASIL VINAIGRETTE

Prepare the basil-flavored vinegar and basil-flavored oil used in this recipe at least two weeks prior to serving. For best fragrance and flavor, combine oil and vinegar just before using to make only enough vinaigrette for immediate use.

2 bunches large-leafed field-grown basil, or 4 bunches
   small-leafed greenhouse-grown basil
1 quart extra-virgin olive oil
1 bottle (about 17 fluid ounces) pear vinegar (available
   in gourmet stores)
Kosher salt
Seasoned pepper (see note)

Wash basil, trimming off any roots. Divide the basil into 2 crocks.

Gently heat olive oil to tepid (90° F), pour over one crock of basil, and let stand until oil is completely cooled and saturated with basil flavor, several hours or overnight, then strain oil through a fine sieve, pressing any remaining oil from basil leaves. Decant oil and store at room temperature in a tightly sealed container for up to 2 months.

Pour vinegar into a saucepan, reserving bottle. Bring vinegar to a simmer over low heat and pour over second crock of basil, cover with cheesecloth, and store for 10 days to 2 weeks. Sterilize vinegar bottle. Strain steeped vinegar into bottle, cork, and store at room temperature.

To make vinaigrette, pour desired amount of basil vinegar into a glass jar. Add salt and seasoned pepper to taste, then add basil oil in a ratio of one-third vinegar to two-thirds oil. Cover jar tightly and shake to emulsify ingredients. Taste and adjust seasonings.

Makes about 6 cups.

NOTE: Seasoned pepper is a mixture of black and white peppercorns, allspice berries, and coriander seeds all ground together; it is available in quality markets.

SEA BASS RAVIOLI IN SAGE BUTTER

1/2 medium-sized onion, sliced
Juice of 1/2 lemon
3/4 cup dry white wine
Salt
3 5-ounce sea bass steaks
10 ounces Swiss chard, minced
2 tablespoons minced shallots
1/3 cup plus 2 tablespoons unsalted butter
3 anchovy fillets
1/2 cup less 1 tablespoon ricotta cheese
1 egg
2 tablespoons freshly grated Parmesan cheese, preferably
   imported parmigiano-reggiano
Seasoned pepper (see note under Basil Vinaigrette)
1 package (about 6 dozen) wonton skins, or pasta
   dough (see note)
24 fresh sage leaves, or 2 teaspoons crumbled dried
   sage leaves
6 quarts water

Prepare a court bouillon by combining onion, lemon juice, wine, a pinch of salt, and enough water to cover fish in a sauté pan or skillet. Bring to simmer over medium-high heat, add fish, cover, reduce heat to simmer, and poach just until fish flakes with a fork. Remove fish from liquid to prevent overcooking.

Gently pan-steam minced chard and shallots in 2 tablespoons butter, adding 1 tablespoon water if needed, until vegetables are soft. Mash and chop anchovies, add to vegetables, and mix well. Add ricotta, egg, Parmesan cheese, and seasoned pepper to taste; blend thoroughly. Taste and adjust seasoning. If not salty enough, add a little more mashed anchovy.

Salad of young greens with sweet peppers and fennel in vinaigrette made of oil and vinegar both steeped with fresh basil.

Parchment packages are opened at the table to reveal veal chop cooked with wild mushrooms, leeks, and herbs.

Lay wonton skins on work surface. Spoon about ½ teaspoon filling into center of each of 36 wonton skins. Run a moistened finger over edges and apply another skin over filling, pressing edges to seal.

Melt remaining ⅓ cup butter in a baking pan. Add sage leaves and place in a 150° F oven.

Bring water to a rolling boil. Lower heat to just under a rolling boil and cook ravioli a few at a time until *al dente,* about 4 to 5 minutes, tasting one to determine correct timing. Drain well and set in pan of sage butter in oven until all are cooked.

To serve, place 6 ravioli in each of 6 pre-heated plates, add a little sage butter, and serve immediately.

Serves 6.

NOTE: You can make your own pasta using 6 cups semolina or unbleached all-purpose flour, 3 whole eggs, 1 egg yolk, and ¼ cup olive oil. Divide dough into 6 pieces, roll or run through a pasta machine until 1/16-inch thick. Make 6 ravioli at a time. Cover formed ravioli to prevent drying.

Veal Chop en Papillote

1½ leeks, white part only, sliced paper thin
¾ pound fresh chanterelle mushrooms, sliced about
  ¼-inch thick
2 tablespoons unsalted butter
Salt
Freshly ground black pepper
6 12-to 14-ounce veal chops, cut 1½ inches thick
Olive oil
6 squares baking parchment (use full width of roll)
6 fresh lemon thyme sprigs or fennel tops

In a large sauté pan or skillet over medium-high heat, cook leeks and mushrooms in butter until liquid evaporates. Season to taste with salt and pepper; reserve.

Set broiler to highest temperature for 15 minutes.

Brush veal chops with olive oil and set on a rack in a broiler pan and broil for 5 minutes. Salt cooked side and broil other side for 5 minutes. Remove from broiler and let cool. Lower oven temperature to 450°F.

Fold parchment squares in half and cut into heart shapes. Butter center of each half. Lay a cooled chop on center of one half of each heart. Evenly distribute sautéed leek and mushroom mixture to cover chops. Add a sprig of chosen herb. Fold papers closed, starting at center of each heart and folding edges a little at a time, overlapping each fold. Fold point of each heart several times to secure contents.

Place packages on a baking sheet and bake under preheated broiler until paper is puffed up and nicely colored, about 8 minutes. Serve immediately with packages intact for diners to open at table with tip of a steak knife.

NOTE: If chanterelles are not available, substitute any wild mushrooms in season: *porcini* or *cepes*, *matsutakes*, or the cultivated *shiitake* or oyster mushroom, or even the common supermarket mushroom.

Serves 6.

Coeur à la crème with Berry Purée

6 squares 8 x 8-inch cheesecloth
Ice water with cubes
1 tablespoon freshly squeezed lemon juice
1 pinch baking soda
8 ounces cream cheese
½ cup powdered sugar
1 pinch salt
1 vanilla bean
1 cup heavy cream
2 pints fresh strawberries or raspberries, stemmed

Soak cheesecloths in ice water to cover, lemon juice, and baking soda.

Beat cream cheese until it is very light and fluffy. Sift powdered sugar into cheese, add salt, and beat well. Scrape seeds from vanilla bean into mixture and mix well.

In a chilled bowl sitting in ice, whip cream just until it holds its shape. Add whipped cream to cream cheese mixture and whisk lightly until thoroughly blended.

Wring each cheesecloth out thoroughly and line heart-shaped molds (see note). Fill molds to somewhat heaping with cheese mixture. Carefully fold ends of cloth over top of cheese. Set molds on a rack inside a pan and refrigerate for a minimum of 6 hours, to drain. (This may be done a day or two in advance).

Reserve a few whole berries for garnish, then purée remainder in a food processor and pass them through a sieve to remove seeds.

To serve, unmold cheese hearts onto serving plates and spoon berry purée around them. Garnish with whole berries.

Serves 6.

NOTE: Coeur à la crème molds (baskets or pierced porcelain hearts) are available from any good culinary supply shop.

WSB&G's Shaken Bloody Mary.

C.B.A. per WSB&G

1 cup plus 2 tablespoons brandy
2 tablespoons anisette liqueur
6 cups hot black coffee
6 lemon zest strips

Combine brandy, anisette, and coffee in a coffee-pot or warmed pitcher; pour into 6 warm stemmed Irish coffee glasses. Garnish each glass with a strip of lemon zest.

Serves 6.

ZUNI CAFE

WHEN THE ZUNI CAFE was named one of California's twenty-five best restaurants by *California Magazine's* poll of the state's food critics, and then ranked Number 3 in San Francisco by the magazine's touring editors, *San Francisco Chronicle* columnist Herb Caen questioned such praise. Loyal patrons were quick to defend the little restaurant known for its Southwestern motif and devotion to quality and freshness.

After college Billy West traveled around the world, sampling different cuisines. Early in 1979 he opened Zuni as an intimate luncheon cafe, with a small investment of money and a big commitment to fine food. Zuni is West's way of giving a party every day, and views the restaurant as an extension of himself, a way of extending hospitality to many guests.

In 1985, Vince Calcagno became co-owner of the restaurant he had managed since 1981, following various jobs in the banking field and a stint as a waiter at Hayes Street Grill. He sees Zuni as the best way to involve himself in "the germination of California cuisine" and the chance to provide a working environment where employees would be happy.

Chef Kathi Riley Smith has no formal cooking training. After working in several small restaurants in Sacramento, she moved to the Bay Area to work with Judy Rodgers at the Union Hotel in Benicia. Later she did her "graduate work" with Alice Waters at Chez Panisse and Bradley Ogden at Campton Place. Her food philosophy? "Keep it simple and honest."

Chef Kathi Riley Smith's Menu for Ten

Margarita

□

Corn Soup with Roasted Sweet Pepper Cream

□

Caesar Salad

□

Braised Rabbit with Bacon, Mustard, and Honey

Buttered Noodles

Navarro Viney, Anderson Valley, 1983

□

Rare-roasted Spiced Filet of Beef   Ratatouille

Acacia Madonna, Napa, 1982

□

Dried Fruits Poached in Armagnac
with Vanilla Ice Cream

OPPOSITE: *Interior features Southwestern motif.* ABOVE: *Corn soup is topped off with roasted sweet pepper cream.*

Left to right: Sous chefs Tara Wolf and Mark Elkin, chef Kathi Riley Smith, pastry chef Julia Bycraft Cookenboo, and owner Billy West.

MARGARITA

2 cups Cuervo white tequila
1 cup Cointreau liqueur
1 cup freshly squeezed lime juice
Kosher salt (optional)

Combine ingredients in a cocktail shaker over ice. Shake and pour into cocktail glasses that have been rimmed with kosher salt if desired.

Serves 10.

Owner Vince Calcagno.

CORN SOUP WITH ROASTED SWEET PEPPER CREAM

3 medium-sized yellow onions, chopped
4 tablespoons unsalted butter
About 15 to 20 ears fresh corn, enough for 10 to 12
  cups cut kernels, cobs reserved
½ gallon milk
4 cups water
Fresh or dried thyme leaves
Bay leaves
Cayenne pepper
2 large red sweet peppers
Salt
Freshly ground black pepper
¾ cup heavy cream

In a large pot over medium-high heat, cook onions in butter until translucent, about 5 minutes, then add corn and cook briefly, about 2 minutes. Add milk, water, reserved cobs, and thyme, bay, and cayenne to taste. Simmer very slowly, without boiling, for about 20 minutes.

Broil sweet peppers until evenly charred on outside. Place in a loosely closed paper bag for 15 minutes, then rub charred skins away. Seed and devein peppers, cut into pieces, and purée in a blender or food processor until smooth. Allow to cool.

Remove and discard cobs from soup. Purée soup in a blender or food processor, straining into another pot to keep warm. Season to taste with salt and pepper.

Whip cream until barely set, fold in cooled pepper purée, and season to taste with salt and pepper.

To serve, ladle soup into warmed bowls and float pepper cream on top. Garnish with ground black pepper.

Serves 10 to 12

CAESAR SALAD

5 heads romaine lettuce
5 whole salt-packed anchovies
2 to 3 eggs
1⅓ to 1½ cups fruity olive oil
4 to 6 garlic cloves, minced or pressed
6 slices French bread, trimmed of crusts and cut into
  ¾-inch cubes
Juice of 2 lemons
Kosher salt
Freshly ground black pepper
¾ cup freshly grated Parmesan

Wash lettuce by immersing in cool water. Discard tough outer leaves and spin small inner leaves (hearts) dry. Wrap in damp kitchen towels and refrigerate until ready to assemble.

Rinse anchovies in cold water. Fillet and drain on a paper towel. Mince and reserve.

Preheat oven to 350° F.

Boil eggs for 1 minute, then place immediately in ice water. Crack, reserve yolks, and save whites for another use.

To make croutons, combine ⅓ cup oil with 1 to 2 cloves minced garlic and toss with bread. Spread on a baking sheet and bake until light brown. Remove from oven and reserve.

To assemble, place remaining 3 to 4 cloves minced garlic with reserved anchovies and egg yolks in bottom of a large bowl. Whisk to blend. Slowly begin adding remaining 1 to 1¼ cups oil, whisking to emulsify with egg and adding lemon juice gradually. Consistency should be light and creamy, not as thick as mayonnaise. Add chilled lettuce leaves and season to taste with salt and pepper. Toss gently so all leaves are well coated. Arrange on chilled plates and sprinkle with reserved croutons and Parmesan.

Serves 10.

BRAISED RABBIT WITH BACON, MUSTARD, AND HONEY

5 2- to 2½-pound frying rabbits
2 tablespoons juniper berries
1 bunch fresh thyme
8 to 10 bay leaves
Grated zest of 2 lemons
Kosher salt
Freshly ground black pepper
2 cups finely chopped carrots
2 cups finely chopped celery
2 cups finely chopped white onions
½ cup olive oil
2 quarts homemade rabbit or chicken stock or canned
  low-sodium chicken broth
½ pound pepper bacon or any other good bacon
¼ cup unfiltered honey
¼ cup Dijon-style mustard
Fresh or dried thyme leaves
Chopped fresh parsley (garnish)

Disjoint each rabbit into 6 pieces and place in one layer in a plastic tub or stainless steel pan.

In a nonreactive bowl, make a marinade by combining juniper berries, thyme, bay leaves, lemon zest, and salt and pepper to taste. Add carrots, celery, and onions and pour over rabbit. Cover with plastic and marinate 2 to 3 days in refrigerator. When ready to prepare, remove rabbit from refrigerator and let it come to room temperature. Remove rabbit from marinade, drain, and dry with paper towels, reserving marinade.

Preheat oven to 375° F.

Heat olive oil in a heavy-bottomed sauté pan or skillet over medium-high heat, brown rabbit pieces on all sides, and transfer to a large roasting pan. Pour marinade over rabbit. Heat stock in a saucepan and pour over rabbit. Cover pan with foil and braise in oven until rabbit is pink just at the bone, about 40 minutes.

While rabbit is braising, cut bacon into ½-inch pieces and cook until fat is rendered and bacon is slightly browned. Strain off fat and reserve bacon.

Large-scale bouquets feature exotic flowers and leaves.

Remove rabbit from oven and strain 2 to 3 cups braising liquid into a bowl. Reserve.

To make sauce, place bacon in a sauté pan or skillet over medium heat and warm gently, then add reserved braising liquid, honey, mustard, and thyme to taste. Cook until slightly reduced.

Place rabbit on warm dinner plates and pour sauce over it. Sprinkle with chopped parsley and serve with buttered noodles.

Serves 10 to 12.

Rare-roasted spiced filet of beef served with ratatouille.

RARE-ROASTED SPICED FILET OF BEEF

1 aged whole beef filet or tenderloin
1 tablespoon kosher salt
1/3 cup white peppercorns
3 tablespoons black peppercorns, preferably Tellicherry
3 tablespoons whole fennel seeds
1 tablespoon dried lavender
1/4 cup olive oil

Two days before you plan to serve, very carefully remove all fat and sinew from filet. Sprinkle with salt and allow juices to come to surface, about 20 minutes. Coarsely grind each spice separately and combine in a small mixing bowl. Press spice mixture into beef on all sides and marinate in refrigerator for approximately 48 hours. Remove meat from refrigerator and allow it to come to room temperature before cooking.

Preheat oven to 425° F.

Heat olive oil almost to smoking point in a large heavy-bottomed sauté pan or skillet over high heat and place meat gently in pan. Let brown completely on one side, then turn and brown all sides.

Remove from pan and place in a roasting pan in oven until internal temperature reaches 100° F, about 12 minutes. Remove from oven and place beef on carving board to catch all juices. Allow to rest for 5 to 8 minutes before slicing.

Serve with *ratatouille,* or with asparagus and roasted new potatoes.

Serves 10 to 14.

DRIED FRUITS POACHED IN ARMAGNAC WITH VANILLA ICE CREAM

(Julia Bycraft Cookenboo, pastry chef)

1 cup Armagnac
1 cup water
3 tablespoons sugar
Zest of 1/2 orange, cut into thin strips
1 3-inch piece cinnamon stick
2 whole cloves
2/3 cup dried apricot halves, preferably unsulphured
2/3 cup dried figs, preferably white, halved and stems removed
2/3 cup pitted prunes
3 tablespoons raisins
Vanilla ice cream

Combine Armagnac, water, sugar, and orange zest in a nonreactive saucepan. Tie cinnamon stick and cloves in a piece of cheesecloth and add to liquid. Heat to a simmer.

If using unsulphured apricots, add to simmering liquid and cook 5 minutes before adding figs and cooking 10 minutes more. If apricots are sulphured (therefore softer), add along with figs and simmer 10 minutes. Add prunes and simmer 5 minutes more. Add raisins and cook 2 to 3 minutes more. All fruits should now be tender but still holding their shape. Taste poaching liquid and add more sugar or Armagnac to taste

To serve, spoon warm fruits over homemade or high-quality commercial vanilla ice cream. Fruits are rich; small portions are recommended.

Serves 10.

Dried fruits poached in Armagnac are served over vanilla ice cream.

ACKNOWLEDGEMENTS

It takes a lot of talented people to put together a collection such as this. May I offer special thanks and appreciation to the following.

To the chefs of San Francisco's bar & grills for creating menus and sharing recipes, and to the owners, managers, and staff for allowing us to interrupt normal schedules for photography:

Café Bedford: Chef James Murcko and Owner Stephen Tumbas

Campton Place: Chef Bradley Ogden, Pastry Chef Steven Froman, Campton Place Hotel President Bill Wilkinson, Sales Manager Katherine Sullivan, and Marketing Manager Marisa Robbins

Ciao: Chef Tony Chavez, Manager Barbara Beltaire, and Spectrum Foods (also owners of MacArthur Park and Prego), Marketing and Business Development Coordinator Pat Boomer

Fog City Diner: Chef-owner Cindy Pawlcyn, Owners Bill Higgins and Bill Upsom, and Manager Doug Biederbeck

Gaylord India Restaurant: Chef Peshori Lal and Managers Pushpraj Goswami and Kishore Kripalani

Harris': Chef Goetz Boje, Pastry Chef Jean-Ives Charon, Manager Joey Buhagiar, and Owner Mrs. Jack Harris

Hayes Street Grill: Owners Robert Flaherty, Ann Powning Haskel, Richard Sander, and Patricia Unterman and Maître d'Hôtel Alan Zimmerman

L'Entrecôte de Paris: Owner Alexander Mortazavi and his La Brigade de Cuisine

MacArthur Park: Chef Ed Kasky and Manager Danny Sullivan

Perry's: Chef Nabil Massarweh and Owner Perry Butler

Prego: Chef Robert Estenzo, Pastry Chef Cecile Getty, and Manager Stanley Morris

Rings: Chef-owner Julie Ring, Assistant Diego Michel, Pastry Chef Patti Johnson, and Owner Dennis Ring

Rosalie's: Chefs James G. Felsenthal and Ric O'Connell and Owners Bill Belloli and Bill Miller

Sam's Grill: Chef Peter Lu and Owner Gary Seput

Square One: Chef-owner Joyce Goldstein, Pastry Chef Craig Sutter, and Owner Evan Goldstein

Washington Square Bar & Brill: Chef Richard Oku and Owners Ed and Mary Etta Moose, Sam Deitsch, and Mark Scharchern

Zuni Cafe: Chef Kathi Riley Smith, Pastry Chef Julia Bycraft Cookenboo, Sous Chefs Tara Wolf and Mark Elkin, and Owners Billy West and Vince Calcagno

To Ken Burke and Cort Sinnes for first encouraging me to pursue this book.

To Loni Kuhn, Scottie McKinney, Bea Pixa, and Patricia Unterman for suggesting restaurants that should be included.

To Gene Davis for helping me eat my way through numerous bar & Grills.

To the entire staff of Chronicle Books, especially Larry Smith for believing in the project enough to buy it, Jack Jensen for management and sales, Bill LeBlond for editing, David Barich and Fearn Cutler for production, and Mary Ann Gilderbloom for promotion.

To Tom Tracy for his back-breaking work and beautiful photography, to Barbara Tracy for juggling Tom's schedule and editing thousands of transparencies, and to Chris Saul for superb assistance with photography, even cleaning off plates after shooting.

To Martha McNair for long hours of helpful styling and keeping track of models.

To Tom Ingalls for transforming text and photography into a graphically stunning book.

To Mark Leno and Douglas Jackson of Budget Signs for producing Bar & Grill in neon.

To friends and friends of friends for modeling, often without even getting anything to eat: John Carr, Martha Cassleman, Carolyn Chapin, Lin Cotton, Bill Doughty, Betsy Foster, Larry Heller, Ken and Christine High, Tad and Gail High, Tanya High, Ken High III, Al Horton, Sharilyn Hovind, Douglas Jackson, Toby Kahn, Dorothy Knecht, Bill LeBlond, Mark Leno, Brad Look, David Look, Jane D. Look, Stephen Marcus, Alan May, Marian May, Jason McDill, Martha McNair, Arthur Mejia, Drew Montgomery, John Richardson, Mayuko Saul, Bob and Kristi Spence, Brooksley Spence, Jolene Stevenson, Patti Topel, George Turner, Will and Julia Parish, Jack Porter, Donna Weeks, as well as friends of the restaurant owners, employees, and patrons.

To Addie Prey, Buster Booroo, Joshua J. Chew, and Michael T. Wigglebutt for assisting with every word written and taste-testing many of the recipes.

And especially to my partner Lin Cotton for always keeping me together while I put books together.

DIRECTORY

CAFÉ BEDFORD
761 POST STREET
SAN FRANCISCO, CALIFORNIA
415 928 8361

CAMPTON PLACE
340 STOCKTON STREET
SAN FRANCISCO, CALIFORNIA
415 781 5155

CIAO
230 JACKSON STREET
SAN FRANCISCO, CALIFORNIA
415 928 9500

FOG CITY DINER
1300 BATTERY STREET
SAN FRANCISCO, CALIFORNIA
415 982 2000

GAYLORD INDIA RESTAURANT
GHIRARDELLI SQUARE,
900 NORTH POINT STREET
SAN FRANCISCO, CALIFORNIA
415 771 8822

HARRIS'
2100 VAN NESS AVENUE
SAN FRANCISCO, CALIFORNIA
415 673 1888

HAYES STREET GRILL
324 HAYES STREET
SAN FRANCISCO, CALIFORNIA
415 863 5545

L'ENTRECÔTE DE PARIS
2032 UNION STREET
SAN FRANCISCO, CALIFORNIA
415 931 5006

MACARTHUR PARK
607 FRONT STREET
SAN FRANCISCO, CALIFORNIA
415 398 5700

PERRY'S
1944 UNION STREET
SAN FRANCISCO, CALIFORNIA
415 922 9008

PREGO
2000 UNION STREET
SAN FRANCISCO, CALIFORNIA
415 563 3305

RINGS
1131 FOLSOM STREET
SAN FRANCISCO, CALIFORNIA
415 621 2111

ROSALIE'S
1415 VAN NESS AVENUE
SAN FRANCISCO, CALIFORNIA
415 928 7188

SAM'S GRILL AND SEA FOOD RESTAURANT
374 BUSH STREET
SAN FRANCISCO, CALIFORNIA
415 GArfield 1 0594

SQUARE ONE
190 PACIFIC AVENUE MALL
SAN FRANCISCO, CALIFORNIA
415 788 1110

WASHINGTON SQUARE BAR & GRILL
1707 POWELL STREET
SAN FRANCISCO, CALIFORNIA
415 982 8213

ZUNI CAFE
1658 MARKET STREET
SAN FRANCISCO, CALIFORNIA
415 552 2522

INDEX